Sunset

Quick Meals
...with *Fresh* Foods

By the Editors of Sunset Books and Sunset Magazine

Lane Publishing Co. • Menlo Park, California

In 60 minutes or less . . .

Even the cook on a super-busy schedule can turn out tempting meals; all it takes is a little special know-how. In this book, we give you that know-how, with dozens of recipes for main dishes of every description. Instead of prepackaged convenience products, each recipe uses fresh, good-for-you ingredients. Each one also features suggestions for easy accompaniments to help you create complete, balanced meals for family or friends. Best of all, you can serve each meal less than an hour after you put on your apron.

For her help with photography, we thank Cynthia Scheer. And for their generosity in sharing props for use in our photographs, we extend special thanks to Best of All Worlds, S. Christian of Copenhagen, Inc., House of Today, and William-Sonoma Kitchenware.

Coordinating Editor: **Maureen Williams Zimmerman**

Research & Text: **Elaine Woodard**
Claire Coleman
Joan Griffiths

Design: **Lea Damiano Phelps**

Illustrations: **Sharron O'Neil**

Photography: **Nikolay Zurek**

Photo Editor: **Lynne B. Morrall**

Cover: Bright summer vegetables make colorful accents in our easy recipe for Tarragon Chicken with Vegetables (see page 67). For a quick meal year round, substitute seasonal vegetables of your choice. Photography by Nikolay Zurek. Photo styling by JoAnn Masaoka Van Atta. Food styling by Cynthia Scheer.

Editor, Sunset Books: Elizabeth L. Hogan

Sixth printing March 1990

Contents

Special Features

Kitchen Efficiency

Today's lifestyles put extra demands on the home cook—anyone who doesn't believe it should ask one! Modern schedules require that meals be prepared more quickly than ever before, and modern concern with health dictates that those meals be prepared with fresh, wholesome foods, without too much reliance on convenience products. In addition, there has been a real awakening of interest in food in recent years: people have become more sophisticated about eating, and view food as something to be enjoyed and appreciated—not simply as a means for meeting basic nutritional needs.

For the cook, these trends spell a challenge: to prepare delicious and interesting meals from fresh ingredients, without spending a lot of time in the kitchen. This may sound like a difficult task at first, and many cooks do regard it as a chore. But meal preparation needn't be a burden—in fact, with a little planning, it can become one of life's pleasures.

That's where we come in. The next few pages offer guidelines for kitchen efficiency—tips on how to plan menus and trips to the market, advice on organizing equipment and ingredients, and many other ideas for making your meal preparation smoother and faster.

Following this chapter are recipes for main dishes. Each recipe features simple, easy-to-find ingredients with an emphasis on what's fresh; packaged ingredients— canned tomato sauce, for example—are used only when it would be impractical, in the interest of time, to use their fresh counterparts. With every recipe, we also offer suggestions for quickly prepared or easily purchased accompaniments, so you can expand each main dish into a full, balanced meal. Using our streamlined instructions, you'll be able to turn out dozens of attractive and delicious meals—and you can prepare each one in under an hour.

In the following pages, you'll also find that quick meals needn't be limited in variety. Some foods—such as pasta or egg dishes—are naturals for speedy cooking. But you can also serve chicken, fish, meats, and soups that taste as if they've been simmering all day.

How to organize a kitchen

The primary prerequisite of successful quick meals is a well-organized kitchen. You'll shave valuable minutes from food preparation time if you keep your kitchen supplied with the equipment, utensils, and food staples necessary for quick and easy cooking, and if you arrange them so that the cooking process flows naturally and efficiently.

Most kitchen activities take place within the triangle formed by the three major kitchen centers—the refrigerator, the range, and the sink. Think of each point of the triangle as a separate work area; then plan storage appropriate to each. If you have some extra space, include a food preparation center, as well, with storage for flour and sugar canisters, mixing bowls, small appliances (food processor, blender), cook books, and recipe boxes.

Sink center

Besides the obvious—a sink—this center may include a dishwasher, garbage disposer, and trash compactor, as well as cabinets and drawers. In this area, food is rinsed and trimmed, wastes and recyclables are disposed of or stashed, and dishes are washed and stored.

This is probably where you'll want to keep a chopping board, food preparation utensils, wastebasket, and dishwashing and cleaning supplies. If you have a dishwasher, stow dishes and glassware as close to it as possible—this makes for quick, easy unloading. Paper bags can be conveniently stored underneath the sink.

Cooking center

The range—or cooktop with a separate oven—is the focus of the cooking center, which can also include a microwave or convection oven and several electrical cooking appliances.

In base cabinets, store pots and pans, baking sheets, and other large articles of cookware. Fill any nearby drawers with cooking utensils. You'll also want to keep pot holders and herbs and spices within easy reach.

Refrigerator center

With luck, this center may include a floor-to-ceiling pantry wedged between the refrigerator and the adjacent wall. If you store nonperishable food items near the refrigerator, putting groceries away is a snap. Tuck plastic wrap, foil, plastic bags, and food storage containers in a nearby drawer or cabinet.

Storage tips

Equipment, utensils, and ingredients should all be kept in their own special places, and should always be returned to their slots after use. That way, your hands will automatically go to the right place when you need something—no more hunting through several drawers for a vegetable peeler or a set of measuring spoons when you're in a hurry.

Use logic to determine the location of each item. If you think of your kitchen in terms of centers, it's obvious that things should be kept near where they're used. Here are some specific tips for storage in your kitchen.

- Keep a crock of cooking tools near the stove for easy access while cooking. Standing upright in any kind of wide-mouthed jar should be plenty of wooden spoons, your utility spoon, slotted spoon, spatulas, and wire whisks.

- Stow small utensils such as garlic press and vegetable peeler in miscellany drawers; buy plastic divided trays for easy organizing.

- Store knives near your cutting surface in their own protected place—in a wooden knife block, on a magnetic rack, or in a drawer designed to hold knives in individual slots. Never keep knives in a miscellany drawer where their edges will be dulled by knocking against other tools.

- Pots and pans usually go in cabinets near the stove—but if you prefer, a hanging pot rack is a good idea. Not only does a rack save you lots of cabinet space, but you can find the item you need at a glance, without having to bend down and dig in the recesses of a dark cupboard.

- Store herbs and spices in a dark, cool place to preserve their potency—never keep them in the refrigerator. You can store these seasonings in a rack, on a revolving tiered tray, or in any other type of organizer. Arrange them in alphabetical order, and return them to their places immediately after using.

- Store the items you use most frequently in the easiest-to-reach areas. Cabinets that you need a stepladder to reach or other out-of-the-way storage areas are best reserved for those cooking utensils you use only occasionally, or for picnic supplies, party goods, and extra rolls of paper towels.

- In general, stow cleanup supplies and equipment under or near the sink. Do, however, keep handy a roll of paper towels or a dishcloth for quickly wiping up spills, and a towel for drying your hands.

Equipment: The bare essentials

Cooking efficiently and well doesn't require a kitchen full of gadgets. In fact, extra tools, utensils, and appliances can actually hinder you by creating an overcrowded kitchen, which leads to chaos during cooking.

Pots & pans

Purchase heavy, well-balanced pots and pans with tight-fitting lids—the best quality you can afford.

- 1, 2, and 3-quart pans with lids
- 5 to 6-quart Dutch oven
- 7 to 8-inch frying pan with lid
- 10 to 12-inch frying pan with lid
- Cast iron frying pan
- Omelet pan
- 8-inch square baking pan
- 9-inch square baking pan
- 7 by 11-inch baking pan
- 9 by 13-inch baking pan
- 10 by 15-inch rimmed baking pan
- Pie pan (at least one 9-inch pan)
- Baking sheet (at least one)

Dishes & utensils

It's wise to buy duplicates of items you use frequently, such as measuring cups and spoons.

- Casserole dishes
- Soufflé dish
- Mixing bowls (3 sizes)
- Custard cups (2 sizes)
- Glass measuring cups (1, 2, and 4-cup size)
- Standard cups for dry measure (¼, ⅓, ½, and 1-cup size)
- Colander
- Metal vegetable steamer
- Vegetable peeler
- Cutting boards
- Standard measuring spoons
- Spatulas—narrow, wide, and slotted
- Rubber spatulas
- Wooden spoons
- Utility spoon
- Slotted spoon
- Soup ladle
- Tongs
- 2-tined kitchen fork
- Funnel
- Grater
- Garlic press
- Wire whisks
- Can opener
- Bottle opener

- Wine opener
- Pastry brush
- Pot holders
- Kitchen timer
- Lemon zester (optional)

Knives

Purchase good quality knives; store them properly (see page 5), and keep all but the serrated knife sharp with a sharpening steel.

- French knife
- Paring knife
- Serrated knife (bread knife)
- Sharpening steel
- Utility knife (optional)
- Slicing knife (optional)
- Kitchen scissors (optional)

Useful electrical equipment

These devices will enable you to perform many kitchen tasks with reduced time and effort.

- Toaster
- Blender
- Food processor
- Electric mixer
- Microwave oven

Staple foods for quick meals

Always keep a well-stocked larder, and replenish your supplies *before* they run out.

In the refrigerator

These ingredients should stock the shelves and crisper unit of your refrigerator.

- Milk
- Half-and-half (light cream)
- Whipping cream
- Sour cream
- Plain yogurt
- Butter or margarine
- Cheeses (Cheddar, jack, Parmesan, Swiss, cream cheese)
- Eggs
- Mayonnaise
- Catsup
- Chili sauce
- Prepared mustard
- Dijon mustard
- Horseradish
- Granulated beef or chicken stock base
- Bottled lemon juice

- Salad greens
- Tomatoes
- Carrots
- Celery
- Green onions
- Parsley
- Thin-skinned potatoes
- Nuts (peanuts, cashews, walnuts, almonds)

In the produce bin

These don't need refrigeration, but they should be kept in a cool, dark, dry place.

- Apples
- Bananas
- Lemons
- Oranges
- Garlic
- Yellow and red onions
- Russet potatoes

In the freezer

Keep out-of-season fruit and hard-to-find vegetables in the freezer, so you'll have them when you need them. Breads also keep best when frozen—unless you use them very quickly.

- Ice cream
- Raspberries
- Blueberries
- Peaches
- Orange juice concentrate
- Chinese pea pods
- Peas
- Corn
- Green beans
- Breads (white, whole wheat, rye, pumpernickel, English muffins, bagels, dinner rolls)

On the pantry shelf

These canned, bottled, and packaged goods are used frequently in the recipes in this book.

- Canned tomatoes (regular and Italian-style)
- Tomato sauce
- Tomato paste
- Tomato juice
- Tuna
- Chopped clams
- Whole and sliced ripe olives
- Whole and diced green chiles
- Water chestnuts
- Kidney beans
- Pineapple chunks and slices in their own juice
- Sliced pimentos
- Anchovy fillets
- Marinated artichoke hearts

- Major Grey chutney
- Honey
- Peanut butter
- Hoisin sauce
- Soy sauce
- Worcestershire sauce
- Liquid hot pepper seasoning
- Clam juice
- Regular-strength beef or chicken broth (or bouillon cubes)
- Dry sherry
- Marsala
- Wine for cooking (red and white)
- Salad oil
- Olive oil
- Vinegar (white distilled, red wine, white wine)
- Long-grain white rice
- Cracked wheat (bulgur)
- Spaghetti and other pasta
- All-purpose flour
- Sugar (granulated, brown, powdered)
- Salt
- Cornstarch
- Cornmeal
- Fine dry bread crumbs
- Raisins
- Sweet pickle relish
- Shredded coconut
- Semisweet chocolate

In the spice rack

On page 5 you'll find information on proper storage of herbs and spices.

- Dry basil
- Bay leaves
- Caraway seeds
- Chili powder
- Ground cinnamon
- Ground cloves
- Ground cumin
- Curry powder
- Dill weed
- Garlic powder
- Garlic salt
- Ground ginger
- Marjoram leaves
- Dry mint
- Dry mustard
- Ground nutmeg
- Oregano leaves
- Paprika
- Ground pepper (black, white, and red)
- Poppy seeds
- Dry rosemary
- Savory leaves
- Sesame seeds
- Dry tarragon
- Thyme leaves

Efficient planning, shopping & cooking

Almost always, wasted time in the kitchen is a result of inadequate planning. A few minutes taken to organize your menus, plan your shopping, and understand your recipes can save much time and prevent much frustration as meal-time draws near.

Planning menus on a day-to-day basis is inefficient; it forces you to spend extra time thinking about what to cook, and extra time in the supermarket. Instead, plot out a week's worth of menus at a time and do your shopping all at once. (This also allows cost-conscious cooks to take advantage of weekly specials at the market.)

When planning menus and when cooking, always keep simplicity in mind. But consider as well the nutritional content, flavor, texture, and appearance of the food. Remember the following tips; they'll help when you sit down to plan menus that are simple and quick to prepare, yet nutritious and interesting to eat.

- Provide an interesting variety of color, flavor, shape, temperature, and texture in the foods you arrange together in a menu. Combine something crisp with something chewy or something soft; something hot with something refreshingly cool. This way, even if you have time to prepare only one dish, you can create an interesting meal by using contrast—for example, with a hot, robustly seasoned soup, you could serve a cool salad of sliced cucumbers and tomatoes, and crisp bread sticks for a delightful repast.

- When you're planning to cook two or three dishes at once, use different cooking techniques. You wouldn't want to serve sautéed fish with stir-fried vegetables; there would be too much simultaneous activity on the range, all just before serving time. Instead, pair baked fish with the stir-fried vegetables; you can pop the fish into the oven, then turn your full attention to the side dish on the range without feeling harried.

- Plan ahead for leftovers. If you have time to cook a roast on Sunday night, buy a little more than you need; then, on Tuesday night, you might use the leftover meat in a quick main-dish salad or sandwich. Leftover cooked vegetables can be added to salads for extra flavor and texture; leftover steamed rice is good in many soups, or it can be transformed into a main-dish fried rice (see page 51). When planning your menus, remember to consider this kind of creative efficiency.

- Prepare ingredients ahead of time whenever possible, to save valuable minutes during meal preparation. Hard-cook several eggs at once and keep them in the refrigerator for use in salads or school lunches. Shred cheese and keep it refrigerated in glass jars. Wash, dry, and store salad greens as soon as you bring them home from the market.

- Schedule your meals for smooth serving, with everything ready at once. Base your schedule on the time you'll serve the meal, and then work backward from serving time, creating a step-by-step plan. (Use written notes, if it helps.) Plan in 10-minute increments, taking into account that some tasks can be dovetailed: you can assemble the salad while heating the rolls, or chop vegetables while cooking the rice.

We all work at a different pace, so experience is the best guide. Do be sure to allow time for setting the table and assembling serving dishes.

- Use cooking equipment sparingly. The fewer utensils you use, the fewer you'll have to wash after eating. Think about efficiency—whenever you can, let the same bowl serve for two purposes, rather than using two different bowls. And if you're combining small quantities of wet and dry ingredients, just stir them together in the glass cup used to measure the liquid; there's no need to get out a separate mixing bowl.

Before you begin to cook

An organized cook follows a simple, yet essential procedure every time he or she walks into the kitchen to prepare a meal. To avoid last-minute panic, you should adopt this practice, too; before you know it, it will become an automatic part of your meal preparation schedule. Here's what to do:

1. Read the recipe or recipes carefully.

2. Assemble all ingredients you'll need. If you're missing one, check the emergency substitution chart on page 9 to see if you can make a substitution.

3. Get out the pots and pans you'll need, as well as the necessary serving plates and utensils.

4. Set the table (or ask another member of the household to do it for you).

5. Begin cooking, starting with the part of the meal that takes longest to prepare.

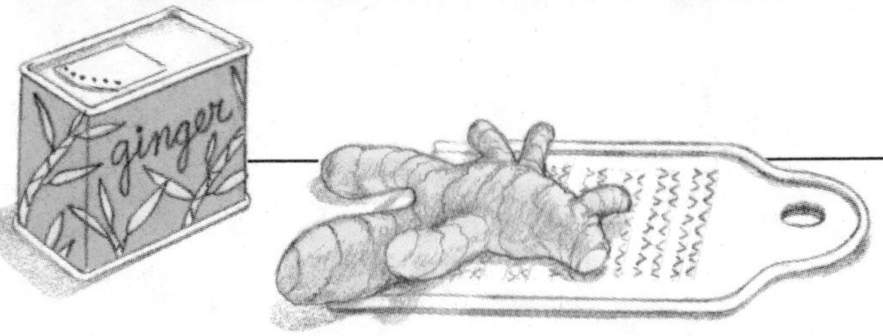

Emergency Substitutions

It's always best to use the exact ingredients called for in a recipe. But if you're in the middle of cooking and find you don't have a particular ingredient on hand, look below for a substitute that will give satisfactory results. We recommend that you avoid making more than one substitution in a single recipe, though.

Ingredient	Substitution
¼ cup fine dry bread crumbs	1 slice crisp dry bread, crushed
1 cup regular-strength chicken or beef broth	1 chicken or beef bouillon cube plus 1 cup hot water
1 cup catsup or tomato-based chili sauce	1 can (8 oz.) tomato sauce plus ½ cup granulated sugar and 2 tablespoons white vinegar
6 squares (6 oz.) semisweet chocolate	1 cup (6 oz.) semisweet chocolate chips
1 tablespoon cornstarch (used for thickening)	2 tablespoons all-purpose flour
½ pint (1 cup) whipping cream (in soups and sauces)	¾ cup milk plus ⅓ cup butter or margarine, melted and cooled
1 clove garlic	⅛ teaspoon garlic powder
½ teaspoon grated fresh ginger	¼ teaspoon ground ginger
1 teaspoon Italian herb seasoning	¼ teaspoon *each* dry basil, marjoram leaves, oregano leaves, and thyme leaves
1 teaspoon grated fresh lemon peel or zest of 1 lemon	1 teaspoon dry lemon peel (purchased)
1 cup milk	½ cup evaporated milk plus ½ cup water, or ⅓ cup powdered whole milk stirred into 1 cup water
1 teaspoon dry mustard	1 tablespoon prepared mustard (except in dry mixtures)
1 medium-size onion	2 teaspoons onion powder
¼ cup minced fresh onion	1 tablespoon instant minced onion (let stand in liquid as directed)
1 teaspoon grated fresh orange peel or zest of 1 orange	1 teaspoon dry orange peel (purchased)
2 tablespoons minced fresh parsley	1 tablespoon dehydrated parsley flakes
2 tablespoons chopped green or red pepper	1 tablespoon sweet pepper flakes (let stand in liquid as directed)
¼ cup dry sherry	¼ cup sweet white wine or Marsala
1 can (1 lb.) tomatoes	2½ cups chopped, peeled, fresh tomatoes, simmered for about 10 minutes
1 cup tomato juice	½ cup tomato sauce plus ½ cup water

Full-meal Soups

For greater efficiency:

Use stock substitutes. Today, you can find rich stock flavor in convenient cubes and envelopes, in jars of granulated bouillon or stock base, and in cans of ready-to-use chicken or beef broth. To substitute one for the other, use 1 cube, 1 envelope, or 1 teaspoon of stock base dissolved in 1 cup hot water to equal 1 cup of homemade stock or ready-to-use canned broth.

Choose between bowls and mugs. There are no fixed rules for choosing serving containers—but deep bowls are best for broths or thin soups that cool quickly, such as Reuben Soup (page 14). And many people enjoy sipping soup from a mug. Wide, shallow bowls suit thick, heat-retaining soups such as Chili Beef Soup (page 14).

Garnish for pizzazz. Just about anything goes as a garnish, but here are a few ideas: a dollop of sour cream or yogurt, a pat of butter, chopped chives or parsley, sliced green onion or black olives, chopped fresh herbs, sliced almonds, lemon or orange slices, crumbled cooked bacon, small cooked shrimp, grated cheese, crisp seasoned croutons.

You can sprinkle garnishes over bubbling hot soup in a tureen or into individual bowls. Or pass toppings at the table and let diners garnish their own bowlfuls. (This is the best way to serve garnishes of cheese or croutons—unless you sprinkle them over the soup just before serving, you may end up with stringy cheese or soggy croutons.)

Store homemade soup. Let hot soup cool, uncovered, in the refrigerator; then cover and keep refrigerated for up to 3 days. For longer storage, ladle cooled soup into glass jars or freezer containers, making sure to leave at least 1 inch of air space at the top of the container to allow for expansion. Close containers airtight and label before freezing; use within 3 months. Thaw frozen soup in the refrigerator overnight; then reheat over medium heat, stirring occasionally. Never try to rush the reheating of soup—it needs to heat evenly. This is especially true of soups made with milk, cream, or cheese, in which ingredients may separate.

Cold Shrimp & Cream Cheese Soup

Zesty and refreshing

To complete the meal, we suggest buttered toasted bagels and fresh fruit.

- 1 bottle (1 qt.) clam-flavored tomato cocktail or tomato juice
- ½ cup chopped peeled cucumber
- ⅓ cup thinly sliced green onions (including tops)
- ¼ pound small cooked shrimp
- 2 tablespoons red wine vinegar
- 2 tablespoons olive oil or salad oil
- 1 tablespoon sugar
- 1 teaspoon dill weed
- 1 clove garlic, minced or pressed
- 1 small package (3 oz.) cream cheese, cut into ¼-inch cubes
- 1 medium-size avocado, pitted, peeled, and diced
- ¼ to ½ teaspoon liquid hot pepper seasoning

In a bowl, combine tomato cocktail, cucumber, onions, shrimp, vinegar, oil, sugar, dill, garlic, cream cheese, and avocado. Stir well to blend; then stir in hot pepper seasoning. Cover and refrigerate for 30 minutes. Makes 4 servings.

Gazpacho with Ham

A tomato-vegetable salad — in soup form

To complete the meal, we suggest cheese bread and melon wedges.

Hint for the cook: You can make this soup ahead, then cover and refrigerate for up to 2 days.

- 4 cups tomato juice
- 3 tablespoons olive oil or salad oil
- 2 tablespoons white wine vinegar
- ½ teaspoon oregano leaves
- 1 small onion, chopped
- ½ green pepper, seeded and chopped
- 1 cucumber, peeled, seeded, and chopped
- 2 tomatoes, seeded and diced
- 1 package (8 oz.) cooked ham, cut into julienne strips (about 1½ cups *total*), or 1½ cups diced cold cooked chicken
- 1 avocado, pitted, peeled, and diced
  Seasoned croutons (optional)

In a large bowl, combine tomato juice, oil, vinegar, and oregano; stir well. Add onion, pepper,

cucumber, tomatoes, ham, and avocado; stir until well combined. Cover and refrigerate for 30 minutes (or longer; see "Hint for the cook"). Serve cold. If desired, pass croutons at the table to spoon over individual servings. Makes 4 servings.

Lentil Vegetable Soup

A colorful vegetable mélange in beefy broth

To complete the meal, we suggest cucumbers and lettuce with vinaigrette dressing, and whole wheat rolls.

Hint for the cook: For a heartier soup, slice three or four frankfurters or smoked link sausages into the broth just before you add the tomatoes; cook the soup a little longer to allow the meat to heat through.

- 2 tablespoons salad oil
- 1 large onion, chopped
- 1 clove garlic, minced or pressed
- 3 carrots, thinly sliced
- 2 stalks celery, thinly sliced
- ½ teaspoon chili powder
- 5 cups regular-strength beef broth or 5 beef bouillon cubes dissolved in 5 cups hot water
- 1 cup lentils
- 1 can (about 1 lb.) stewed tomatoes
  Chopped parsley
  Grated Parmesan cheese

Heat oil in a 4-quart pan over medium-high heat. Add onion and garlic and cook, stirring occasionally, until soft (about 5 minutes). Add carrots, celery, and chili powder; cook, stirring, for 1 to 2 more minutes. Add broth and lentils and bring to a boil; cover, reduce heat, and simmer until lentils are tender (about 35 minutes).

Just before serving, stir tomatoes into soup; cook until heated through (about 1 more minute). Sprinkle with parsley; pass cheese at the table to spoon over individual servings. Makes 4 to 6 servings.

Beer & Cheese Soup

Smooth, cheesy soup dotted with vegetables

To complete the meal, we suggest a marinated bean salad, cherry tomatoes, and crusty rolls.

> 6 tablespoons butter or margarine
> ½ cup *each* thinly sliced celery, diced carrot, and chopped onion
> 6 tablespoons all-purpose flour
> ½ teaspoon dry mustard
> ¼ teaspoon thyme leaves
> 2 cans (14½ oz. *each*) regular-strength chicken broth
> 1½ cups (6 oz.) shredded sharp Cheddar cheese
> 2 tablespoons grated Parmesan cheese
> 1 can (12 oz.) beer, at room temperature
> Salt and pepper

In a 3-quart pan over medium-high heat, melt butter. Add celery, carrot, and onion; cook for 5 minutes. Stir in flour, mustard, and thyme; bring to a boil and boil for 1 minute. Remove from heat and gradually stir in broth. Return to heat and cook, stirring, until mixture boils; cover, reduce heat, and simmer for 15 minutes. Add Cheddar cheese, a handful at a time, stirring until blended; stir in Parmesan. After all cheese has been incorporated, stir in beer and cook until soup is heated through (about 1 more minute). Season to taste with salt and pepper. Makes 4 servings.

Clam & Corn Chowder

Creamed corn adds texture to a light entrée

To complete the meal, we suggest a raw vegetable plate, crisp crackers, and chocolate cake.

> Condiments: Crumbled crisp bacon, hulled sunflower seeds, seasoned croutons, sliced green onions (including tops)
> 2 tablespoons butter or margarine
> 1 small onion, chopped
> 2 cans (6½ oz. *each*) chopped clams
> 1 bottle (8 oz.) clam juice
> 1 can (about 17 oz.) cream-style corn
> 1 cup milk
> ¼ teaspoon liquid hot pepper seasoning

Prepare 2 or more condiments of your choice, placing each in an individual bowl; set aside.

In a 4-quart pan over medium heat, melt butter. Add onion and cook, stirring occasionally, until soft (about 5 minutes). Stir in clams and their liquid, clam juice, corn, milk, and hot pepper seasoning; cook, stirring occasionally, until heated through (about 10 minutes). At the table, pass condiments to sprinkle over individual servings. Makes 4 servings.

Fish Chowder

A rib-sticking chowder with vegetables

To complete the meal, we suggest a spinach salad and crusty rolls.

> ¼ pound salt pork, diced
> 1 large onion, chopped
> 1 pound red thin-skinned potatoes, cubed
> 2 bottles (8 oz. *each*) clam juice
> 1 can (14½ oz.) regular-strength chicken broth
> 1 bay leaf
> 2 pounds fish fillets (rockfish, ling cod, or turbot), cut into 1½-inch squares
> 1 package (about 10 oz.) frozen peas
> 1 package (about 10 oz.) frozen corn
> 1½ cups half-and-half (light cream) or milk
> Salt and pepper
> Chopped parsley

In a 5-quart Dutch oven over medium-high heat, cook salt pork, stirring frequently, until browned and crisp. Spoon off and discard all but 2 tablespoons drippings. Add onion and cook, stirring occasionally, until soft (about 5 minutes). Stir in potatoes, clam juice, broth, and bay leaf. Bring to a boil over high heat; then cover, reduce heat, and simmer until potatoes are fork-tender (about 15 minutes).

Add fish, frozen peas, and frozen corn. Increase heat to high and return to a boil; cover, reduce heat, and simmer until flesh inside is just opaque when fish is prodded in thickest portion with a fork (5 to 8 minutes). Stir in half-and-half and season to taste with salt and pepper. Cook until heated through (1 to 2 more minutes). Sprinkle with parsley. Makes 6 servings.

Dutch Shrimp Soup

Tender shrimp in a creamy tomato-dill broth

To complete the meal, we suggest a butter lettuce salad, whole grain bread, and fruit and cheese.

- 4 **tablespoons butter or margarine**
- 5 **tablespoons all-purpose flour**
- 1 **can (14½ oz.) regular-strength chicken broth**
- 3 **cups milk**
- ¼ **cup *each* whipping cream and finely chopped parsley**
- 1 **teaspoon *each* paprika and dill weed**
- 3 **tablespoons lemon juice**
- 5 **tablespoons tomato paste**
- 1 **pound small cooked shrimp**

In a 5-quart Dutch oven over medium-high heat, melt butter. Add flour and cook, stirring, until mixture is bubbly. Remove from heat and gradually stir in broth. Return to heat and cook, stirring, until sauce is smooth, thick, and boiling. Stirring constantly, gradually add milk and cream; then stir in parsley, paprika, dill, lemon juice, and tomato paste. Cook just until heated through (2 to 3 minutes). Stir in shrimp and cook for 1 more minute. Makes 4 servings.

Chicken Noodle Soup with Yogurt

A tangy version of a childhood favorite

To complete the meal, we suggest rye bread and fresh fruit of the season.

- 2 **tablespoons salad oil**
- 1 **large onion, chopped**
- 1 **large can (49½ oz.) regular-strength chicken broth**
- 3 **chicken bouillon cubes**
- 3 **cloves garlic, minced or pressed**
- 1 **teaspoon thyme leaves**
- ¼ **teaspoon *each* pepper and dill weed**
- ¼ **cup chopped parsley**
- 3 **small carrots, sliced**
- 6 **ounces wide egg noodles**
- 3 **cups diced cooked chicken**
- 1 **pint (2 cups) plain yogurt**
- 2 **tablespoons cornstarch**
  Sugar (optional)

Heat oil in a 5-quart Dutch oven over medium heat. Add onion and cook, stirring occasionally, until soft (about 5 minutes). Add broth, bouillon cubes, garlic, thyme, pepper, dill, parsley, and carrots. Bring to a boil over high heat; then cover, reduce heat, and simmer until carrots are fork-tender (about 30 minutes). Stir in noodles and cook, uncovered, for 10 minutes. Stir in chicken.

In a bowl, combine yogurt and cornstarch; stir until smooth. Slowly add to soup, stirring until well blended. Bring to a boil over high heat; continue boiling until soup is slightly thickened. Taste and add a little sugar, if needed, to smooth out flavor (brands of yogurt vary in tartness). Makes 4 to 6 servings.

Chicken & Vegetable Soup

Brimming with fresh, lively colors and flavors

To complete the meal, we suggest a fresh fruit salad and crisp crackers or bread sticks.

- 6 **cups regular-strength chicken broth or 6 chicken bouillon cubes dissolved in 6 cups hot water**
- ½ **cup long-grain white rice**
- 3 **medium-size carrots, cut into ⅛-inch slices**
- 3 **stalks celery, cut into ¼-inch slices**
- 2 **small zucchini, cut into ¼-inch slices**
- 6 **tablespoons butter or margarine**
- 6 **tablespoons all-purpose flour**
- 1 **pint (2 cups) half-and-half (light cream) or milk**
- 3 **cups bite-size pieces cooked chicken or turkey**
- ½ **cup thinly sliced green onions (including tops)**
  Salt and pepper
  Minced parsley

In a 5-quart Dutch oven over high heat, bring broth to a boil. Add rice; cover, reduce heat, and simmer for 10 minutes. Add carrots, celery, and zucchini; cover and simmer until vegetables are tender-crisp (about 10 more minutes).

Meanwhile, in a small pan over medium heat, melt butter. Stir in flour and cook, stirring, until mixture is bubbly. Remove from heat and gradually stir in half-and-half; then stir in about 1 cup of the broth from soup mixture. Return to heat and cook, stirring, until sauce is smooth, thick, and boiling. Stir sauce into soup mixture.

Stir in chicken and onions; season to taste with salt and pepper. Cook until heated through (about 1 more minute). Sprinkle with parsley. Makes 4 to 6 servings.

Chili Beef Soup

Hearty, thick soup, accented with fiesta flavors

To complete the meal, we suggest buttered cornbread, a tossed green salad, and ice cream or sherbet.

>   1   **pound lean ground beef**
>   1   **large onion, chopped**
>   3   **cups regular-strength beef broth, or 3 beef bouillon cubes dissolved in 3 cups hot water**
>   1   **can (about 15 oz.) tomato purée**
>   1   **tablespoon chili powder**
>   ½   **teaspoon** *each* **ground cumin and oregano leaves**
>   ¼   **teaspoon garlic powder**
>   2   **cans (about 15 oz.** *each***) kidney beans, drained**
>   1   **can (about 12 oz.) whole kernel corn, drained**
>   **Salt and pepper**
>   ¼ to ½ **cup shredded Cheddar cheese**

Crumble beef into a 5-quart Dutch oven. Add onion and cook over medium-high heat, stirring occasionally, until meat loses its pink color and onion is soft; spoon off and discard fat. Reduce heat; stir in broth, tomato purée, chili powder, cumin, oregano, garlic powder, beans, and corn. Cover and simmer for 30 minutes. Season to taste with salt and pepper. Pass cheese at the table to spoon over individual servings. Makes 4 servings.

Reuben Soup

Mellow sauerkraut broth with Polish sausage chunks

To complete the meal, we suggest buttered black bread, pickles, orange wedges, and beer.

>   1   **tablespoon butter or margarine**
>   6   **kielbasa (Polish sausages—about 2½ lbs.** *total***), cut into ½-inch-thick slices**
>   2   **cans (14½ oz.** *each***) regular-strength beef broth**
>   1   **cup dry white wine or 1 cup regular-strength beef broth**
>   1   **jar or can (about 32 oz.) sauerkraut, rinsed and drained**
>   1½ **teaspoons caraway seeds**
>   2   **bay leaves**

In a 5-quart Dutch oven over medium-high heat, melt butter. Add sausage pieces and cook, stirring occasionally, until evenly browned. Stir in broth, wine, sauerkraut, caraway seeds, and bay leaves; bring to a boil. Reduce heat and simmer,

uncovered, for 10 minutes. Remove bay leaves, then serve. Makes 6 servings.

Italian Sausage Soup

Savory vegetable soup with sausage morsels

Pictured on page 18

To complete the meal, we suggest a green salad, bread sticks, red wine, and Italian cookies.

>   1½ **pounds mild Italian sausages, cut into ½-inch slices**
>   2   **cloves garlic, minced or pressed**
>   2   **large onions, chopped**
>   1   **large can (about 28 oz.) Italian-style tomatoes**
>   3   **cans (14½ oz.** *each***) regular-strength beef broth**
>   1½ **cups dry red wine or water**
>   ½   **teaspoon dry basil**
>   3   **tablespoons chopped parsley**
>   1   **medium-size green pepper, seeded and chopped**
>   2   **medium-size zucchini, cut into ½-inch slices**
>   5   **ounces medium-size bow-shaped noodles (about 3 cups)**
>   **Grated Parmesan cheese**

In a 5-quart Dutch oven over medium-high heat, cook sausage slices until lightly browned on the outside and no longer pink inside when slashed. Remove from Dutch oven with a slotted spoon, drain on paper towels, and set aside. Spoon off and discard all but 3 tablespoons drippings. Add garlic and onions and cook, stirring occasionally, until onions are soft (about 5 minutes).

Stir in tomatoes (break up with a spoon) and their liquid; then add sausage slices, broth, wine, and basil. Bring to a full rolling boil; cover, reduce heat, and simmer for 20 minutes. Stir in parsley, green pepper, zucchini, and noodles. Cover and simmer, stirring occasionally, until noodles are *al dente* (10 to 15 minutes). Skim off and discard fat. Pass cheese at the table to spoon over individual servings. Makes 6 servings.

Timesaver: The Food Processor

The food processor has many uses, and all of them will save you time and energy. Once you get used to using this machine, you'll wonder how you ever got along without it. Here are some ways to put the food processor to work for you.

Shredding & grating cheese

Shredded and grated cheeses are staple ingredients that you can prepare ahead, refrigerate or freeze, and keep on hand for use in recipes. A 4-ounce piece of jack, Swiss, Cheddar, or any other firm cheese will yield 1 cup shredded cheese; for best results, shred these cheeses when they're cold, using the shredding disc. To grate harder cheeses, such as Asiago, Parmesan, and Romano, cut away and discard the tough, hard edges; then cut cheese into 1-inch cubes. Place the metal blade in the work bowl, turn the motor on and drop the cheese, a few pieces at a time, into the feed tube. Continue until all cheese is processed (grated). A 3-ounce wedge will yield ½ cup of finely grated cheese.

For convenient storage, transfer the shredded or grated cheese to glass jars, then cover and refrigerate for up to a week; freeze for longer storage.

Making your own bread crumbs

The food processor makes it easy to prepare fine dry bread crumbs from crisp dried bread, and soft bread crumbs from fresh bread. Place the metal blade in the work bowl, turn the motor on, and drop chunks of bread, a few pieces at a time, into the feed tube. (Don't start the machine with pieces of hard bread already in the work bowl—a piece might become wedged between the processor bowl and the blade, preventing it from turning, and it's time-consuming to remove the work bowl and the blade.)

One sandwich-size slice of crisp dried bread yields ¼ cup fine dry crumbs; one sandwich-size slice of fresh bread yields ½ cup soft crumbs. You can make a large quantity of fine dry crumbs to keep on hand; store in an airtight glass jar on the pantry shelf. Because of the moisture content of fresh bread, soft crumbs mold rapidly and should be used soon after processing.

Chopping vegetables

A few seconds can make the difference between vegetables that are chopped and those that are watery and puréed. Using the on-off technique will always give you evenly chopped vegetables: each time you turn the motor off, the food drops to the bottom of the work bowl, so it will be in the path of the blade when the motor is restarted.

To chop an onion, first cut it into 1½-inch chunks. Place the metal blade in the work bowl and add onion chunks; then give the machine 3 on-off bursts. Scrape down sides. After 2 or 3 more on-off bursts, the onion will be finely chopped.

Use this on-off technique to chop foods that have a fairly high water content—fresh fruits, vegetables such as celery, green onions, green peppers, mushrooms, onions, potatoes, spinach, tomatoes, and zucchini—as well as nuts, hard-cooked eggs, and raw or cooked meat.

Chopping parsley in quantity

For perfectly chopped parsley, remove the stems, then wash and thoroughly dry the sprigs (wet parsley turns to mush). Using the metal blade in the work bowl, process the feathery sprigs continuously until finely chopped. Store chopped parsley, covered, in the refrigerator for up to a week; use in recipes or for garnishes.

Main-dish Salads

For greater efficiency:

Wash greens ahead of time. You can do this as soon as you get home from the market. First remove coarse outer leaves, stems, and cores; then wash leaves and drain on paper towels or a clean dishtowel. Wrap them loosely in dry paper towels or a fresh dishtowel, and store in a plastic bag in the crisper unit of your refrigerator. When you're ready for salad, your greens will be clean, chilled, and crisp.

Prepare a supply of green salad. You can make several days' worth of tossed green salad at one time, then keep it in the refrigerator to accompany the week's main dishes. Tear up salad greens and place in a plastic bag with other crisp vegetables such as sliced radishes, celery, and green pepper. Depending on the type of greens used and their freshness when purchased, your salad will keep for 3 to 5 days.

Plan ahead for cold cooked meats. If you're planning to roast one chicken for Sunday dinner, roast two instead—and use the extra bird for cold meat in main-dish salads. Keep in mind that a 3-pound frying chicken will yield about 3 cups meat; a 1-pound whole chicken breast will yield about 1½ cups meat; and a half a pound of cooked boneless ham, beef, or turkey will yield about 2 cups meat. (You can also buy cold cooked meat at a deli.)

Make dressings in quantity. To avoid last-minute fuss, keep two or three kinds of homemade salad dressings (page 20) in the refrigerator, in enough quantity to dress two or three main-dish salads or several side-dish salads. Dressings made with oil should be brought to room temperature and stirred to blend again before being added to a salad.

Hard-cook eggs in quantity. Keep hard-cooked eggs in the refrigerator (mark them to distinguish them from raw eggs). A common ingredient in main-dish salads, they add extra flavor and a protein boost to side-dish salads. Slice or chop coarsely and add to salad, or cut eggs into wedges to use as a garnish.

Egg Salad Boats

Dilled egg salad heaped into juicy tomato "boats"

To complete the meal, we suggest buttered toast triangles or English muffins, and ripe olives.

  12 **hard-cooked eggs, coarsely chopped**
  ½ **cup mayonnaise**
  1 **cup thinly sliced celery**
  3 **green onions (including tops), thinly sliced**
  ¾ **teaspoon dill weed**
  ½ **teaspoon lemon juice**
  4 **large tomatoes**
    Lettuce leaves

In a large bowl, gently stir together eggs, mayonnaise, celery, onions, dill, and lemon juice until well combined; set aside.

With a small, sharp knife, cut out cores from tomato stem ends; then cut each tomato almost to the base into 8 wedges (don't slice all the way through). Place each on a lettuce-lined plate, carefully spread wedges open, and spoon about ¾ cup egg salad into center. Makes 4 servings.

Shanghai Tofu & Peanut Salad

A high-protein salad with a Chinese accent

To complete the meal, we suggest crisp crackers, fresh fruit, and jasmine tea.

  1 **package (1 lb.) medium-firm (regular) tofu (bean curd)**
    Salad oil
    Sesame Dressing (recipe follows)
  ¾ **pound bean sprouts**
  1 **medium-size cucumber**
  ⅔ **cup shredded carrot**
  3 **green onions (including tops), thinly sliced**
  ¾ **cup coarsely chopped salted peanuts**

Cut tofu crosswise into 1-inch-thick slices. Place in a colander; rinse with cold water and let drain for 10 minutes, then place between paper towels and gently press out excess water. Place tofu on a wire rack in a shallow rimmed baking pan and brush all surfaces with oil.

Bake in a 350° oven for 20 minutes. Let cool, then cut into small, thin strips (about ¼ by ¼ by 1 inch). Prepare Sesame Dressing; add tofu, stirring gently to coat. Set aside.

Drop bean sprouts into a 5 to 6-quart kettle half filled with boiling water. Cook until water resumes a full rolling boil; then drain, rinse with cold water, and drain again.

Peel cucumber, if desired, and cut in half lengthwise. Scoop out and discard seeds (if large); cut into thin slices. Just before serving, add bean sprouts, cucumber, carrot, onions, and peanuts to tofu mixture; toss gently. Makes 4 to 6 servings.

Sesame Dressing. In a large salad bowl, stir together ¼ cup **white wine vinegar,** 2 tablespoons each **sugar** and **salad oil,** 1 tablespoon **soy sauce,** 1½ teaspoons **sesame oil,** ¾ teaspoon **salt,** and ¼ teaspoon **ground red pepper** (cayenne).

Tuna Chutney Salad

Tuna tossed with greens and creamy curry dressing

To complete the meal, we suggest hot buttered rolls and iced tea.

  ½ **cup mayonnaise**
  ⅓ **cup finely chopped Major Grey chutney**
  1 **teaspoon curry powder**
  1 **tablespoon white wine vinegar**
  ¼ **teaspoon ground ginger**
  2 **quarts torn, lightly packed salad greens (spinach, red leaf lettuce, butter lettuce, romaine, or a combination)**
  2 **cups thinly sliced celery**
  ½ **cup thinly sliced green onions (including tops)**
  1 **can (8 oz.) pineapple chunks in their own juice, drained**
  2 **cans (6½ oz. each) chunk-style tuna, drained well and flaked, or 2 to 3 cups diced cooked chicken or turkey**
  ⅔ **cup Spanish peanuts**

In a small bowl, stir together mayonnaise, chutney, curry powder, vinegar, and ginger; set aside. In a large salad bowl, combine greens, celery, onions, pineapple, and tuna. Just before serving, pour dressing over salad and toss to coat greens thoroughly; sprinkle peanuts over top. Makes 4 to 6 servings.

Macaroni Tuna Salad

An ultra-quick Italian pasta salad

To complete the meal, we suggest crisp whole radishes and carrot and celery sticks.

- 1 **package (1 lb.) salad macaroni**
  Boiling salted water
- 2 **cans (12½ oz. each) chunk-style tuna, drained well and flaked**
- ½ **cup olive oil or salad oil**
- ¼ **cup red wine vinegar**
- 2 **cloves garlic, minced or pressed**
- ½ **cup chopped parsley**
- 1 **tablespoon capers (optional)**
- 1 **teaspoon salt**
  Dash of pepper

Following package directions, cook macaroni in a large kettle of boiling salted water until *al dente;* drain, rinse with cold water, and drain again. Meanwhile, in a large bowl, stir together tuna, oil, vinegar, garlic, parsley, capers (if desired), salt, and pepper. Add macaroni and stir until combined. Makes 6 to 8 servings.

Salade Niçoise for Two

A colorful salad from southern France

To complete the meal, we suggest red wine, crusty rolls, and ice cream.

- 4 **small thin-skinned potatoes (about 2 inches in diameter)**
- ¼ **pound green beans, ends removed**
  Spinach leaves
- 2 **cans (3½ oz. each) solid light tuna, drained**
- 4 **anchovy fillets**
  Ripe olives
- 2 **hard-cooked eggs, each cut into quarters**
- ¼ **cup olive oil or salad oil**
- 2 **tablespoons red wine vinegar**
- 1 **clove garlic, minced or pressed**
- ½ **teaspoon Dijon mustard**
  Dash each of salt and pepper

To warm your bones on a wintry night, try hearty Italian Sausage Soup (page 14). It goes well with bread sticks and a big green salad with Creamy Mustard Dressing (page 20).

Place potatoes in a small pan; add water to cover. Place over high heat and bring to a boil; boil, covered, for 15 minutes. Add beans and continue to boil until potatoes are tender throughout when pierced and beans are just tender-crisp to bite (about 6 more minutes). Drain vegetables and rinse under cold running water until cool enough to handle; drain again. Peel potatoes, if desired, and cut into ¼-inch-thick slices.

Line 2 salad plates with spinach leaves. Invert one can tuna onto each plate; arrange anchovies in a crisscross pattern over tuna. Arrange potatoes, beans, eggs, and olives around tuna.

In a small bowl, combine oil, vinegar, garlic, mustard, salt, and pepper. Drizzle dressing evenly over salads. Makes 2 servings.

Shrimp-Rice Salad

Creamy rice salad, chock-full of tender baby shrimp

To complete the meal, we suggest fresh fruit and a cool beverage.

- 1 **cup long-grain white rice**
  Creamy Lemon Dressing (recipe follows)
- ½ **cup sliced almonds**
- 1 **pound small cooked shrimp**
- 1 **cup each thinly sliced celery and chopped green pepper**
- 1 **can (8 oz.) water chestnuts, drained and thinly sliced**
  Salt and pepper
  Lettuce leaves

Cook rice according to package directions. Meanwhile, prepare Creamy Lemon Dressing; then spread almonds in a shallow pan and toast in a 350° oven, stirring occasionally, for about 6 minutes or until golden.

Spread hot rice on a baking sheet and let cool for 30 minutes. Gently stir together cooled rice, shrimp, celery, green pepper, and water chestnuts; add dressing and gently stir until all ingredients are well coated. Season to taste with salt and pepper. Line a platter or 4 individual plates with lettuce leaves; spoon salad atop lettuce and sprinkle with almonds. Makes 4 servings.

Creamy Lemon Dressing. In a small bowl, combine ¾ cup **mayonnaise,** 1 teaspoon **grated lemon peel,** 1 tablespoon **lemon juice,** 2 teaspoons **prepared horseradish,** and ¼ teaspoon **garlic powder.** Stir in ½ cup thinly sliced **green onions** (including tops), ¼ cup chopped **parsley,** and 1 jar (2 oz.) **sliced pimentos** (drained).

Salad Dressings

In just minutes, you can prepare homemade salad dressings to enhance main-dish and side-dish salads alike. Not only do they taste better than bottled dressings, but they contain none of the artificial ingredients often found in purchased products. These recipes make 2 cups or more, so you'll have some left over—refrigerate it and use it the next time you serve salad.

The following dressings can be used on a variety of salads. Keep in mind, though, that thick, creamy dressings such as Thousand Island are more appropriate for crunchier greens, while lighter dressings go well with delicate, leafy greens. And remember that dressings made with oil and refrigerated should be brought to room temperature and stirred to blend again before being added to a salad.

Basic Vinaigrette

In a jar, combine ½ cup **white wine vinegar,** 1 teaspoon **salt,** a dash of **pepper,** and 1½ cups **salad oil** or olive oil (or a combination). Close jar tightly and shake to mix thoroughly. Makes 2 cups.

Creamy Mustard Dressing
Pictured on page 18

In a blender or food processor, combine 2 **egg yolks,** ¼ cup **red wine vinegar,** 2 tablespoons **Dijon mustard,** 1 teaspoon **salt,** ¾ teaspoon **pepper,** and 1 teaspoon **dry tarragon.** Whirl until blended. With motor running gradually add 1½ cups **olive oil** or salad oil in a slow, steady stream about ¹/₁₆ inch wide until all is incorporated. Makes 2 cups.

Chili-spiced Thousand Island Dressing

In a small bowl, stir together 2 cups **mayonnaise,** ½ cup **tomato-based chili sauce,** 2 tablespoons **sweet pickle relish,** 4 teaspoons **lemon juice,** and 1 teaspoon **chili powder** until well blended. Makes 2½ cups.

Sesame Chicken Salad

Delicately flavored and full of crunchy vegetables

Pictured on page 23

To complete the meal, we suggest Won Ton Crispies (page 25) and fresh tangerines or oranges.

- 2 **tablespoons sesame seeds**
- ¼ **cup salad oil**
- 3 **tablespoons lemon juice**
- 1½ **tablespoons** *each* **soy sauce and white wine vinegar**
- 3 **cloves garlic, minced or pressed**
- 2 **teaspoons finely minced fresh ginger**
- ½ **pound edible-pod peas, ends and strings removed, or 1 package (6 oz.) frozen Chinese pea pods, thawed**
- ½ **pound bean sprouts**
- 3 **to 3½ cups shredded cold cooked chicken**

In a small frying pan over medium heat, toast sesame seeds, stirring often, until golden (about 5 minutes); let cool, then place in a large bowl. Add oil, lemon juice, soy, vinegar, garlic, and ginger; set aside.

Drop fresh peas and bean sprouts into a 5 to 6-quart kettle half filled with boiling water. (If using thawed frozen pea pods, just drain them; no need to cook.) Cook until water resumes a full rolling boil; drain, rinse well with cold water, and drain again. Add vegetables and chicken to sesame mixture; stir gently. Makes 4 servings.

Slivered Chicken Liver Salad

An unusual salad featuring chicken livers

To complete the meal, we suggest dinner rolls and fresh fruit of the season.

- ¼ **cup olive oil or salad oil**
- 3 **tablespoons lemon juice**
- ½ **teaspoon** *each* **salt and sugar**
- ¼ **teaspoon** *each* **dry chervil, thyme leaves, and dry mustard**
- ⅛ **teaspoon white pepper**
- 2 **quarts torn, lightly packed curly endive, Australian lettuce, or romaine**
- 1 **small red onion, thinly sliced**
- 1 **cup thinly sliced celery**
- ¼ **cup chopped parsley**
- 1 **tablespoon butter or margarine**
- 1 **tablespoon olive oil or salad oil**
- 1 **pound chicken livers, cut in half**

In a measuring cup, stir together the ¼ cup oil, lemon juice, salt, sugar, chervil, thyme, mustard, and pepper; set aside.

In a large salad bowl, combine endive, onion, celery, and parsley; set aside.

Just before serving, melt butter in the 1 tablespoon oil in a wide frying pan over medium-high heat. Add chicken livers and cook until just firm but still slightly pink in center when slashed (about 5 minutes). Lift livers out and quickly cut into thin slivers. Return to pan and stir to coat with drippings; then pour onto endive mixture. Stir dressing and pour over all; toss to mix well. Makes about 4 servings.

Curried Chicken & Fruit Salad

Refreshing fare for a summer evening

To complete the meal, we suggest crisp finger vegetables, whole wheat toast, and iced tea.

> ½ pint (1 cup) plain yogurt
> 3 tablespoons finely chopped **Major Grey chutney**
> 1 teaspoon *each* curry powder and ground coriander
> ¾ teaspoon garlic salt
> ½ teaspoon dry mustard
> Ground red pepper (cayenne)
> 3 cups bite-size pieces cold cooked chicken or turkey
> 1 small green pepper, seeded and coarsely chopped
> 1 can (11 oz.) mandarin oranges, drained well
> 1 can (8 oz.) pineapple chunks in their own juice, drained well
> ½ cup raisins
> ¼ cup thinly sliced green onions (including tops)
> 2 small bananas
> Butter lettuce leaves
> ½ cup roasted salted peanuts, almonds, or cashews, coarsely chopped

In a small bowl, stir together yogurt, chutney, curry powder, coriander, garlic salt, and mustard. Season to taste with red pepper, adding a pinch at a time; set aside.

In a large bowl, combine chicken, green pepper, oranges, pineapple, raisins, and onions. Cut bananas into ¼-inch-thick slices; stir in. Pour yogurt dressing over mixture and stir gently.

On each of 4 salad plates, arrange 2 or 3 butter lettuce leaves. Distribute chicken salad evenly atop lettuce; sprinkle with peanuts. Makes 4 servings.

Salad Olé

A whole-meal entrée, Mexican style

To complete the meal, we suggest hot buttered tortillas and beer.

Hint for the cook: For a milder flavor, omit chorizo sausage and use all ground beef.

> **Avocado Dressing (recipe follows)**
> 1 quart shredded, lightly packed iceberg lettuce
> 1 can (2¼ oz.) sliced ripe olives, drained
> 1 medium-size cucumber, peeled and sliced
> 1 cup shredded carrot
> 1 can (about 15 oz.) kidney beans, drained
> 1 cup (4 oz.) shredded jack cheese
> ½ pound *each* lean ground beef and chorizo sausage
> 1 large onion, chopped
> 12 cherry tomatoes, halved

Prepare Avocado Dressing; cover and refrigerate while preparing salad.

In a large salad bowl, combine lettuce, olives, cucumber, carrot, beans, and cheese; set aside.

Crumble beef into a wide frying pan. Remove sausage casings and crumble chorizo into pan. Add onion and cook over medium heat, stirring occasionally, until meat is browned and onion is soft. Spoon off and discard fat; then spoon meat mixture over lettuce mixture. Toss gently and garnish with cherry tomatoes. Serve immediately. Pass dressing to spoon over individual portions. Makes 4 to 6 servings.

Avocado Dressing. Peel and pit 1 large ripe **avocado.** Place in a small bowl; mash thoroughly. Stir in 1 tablespoon **lime juice,** 1 can (4 oz.) **diced green chiles,** ¼ teaspoon **ground cumin,** 1½ teaspoons **garlic salt,** and ⅓ cup **regular-strength beef broth.** Mix until smooth.

Sweet & Sour Meatball Salad

Oriental flavors distinguish this whole-meal salad

To complete the meal, we suggest hot tea and a fruit sherbet for dessert.

Sesame Oven Meatballs (recipe follows)
1 small green pepper, seeded and cut into ½-inch-wide strips
2 medium-size carrots, cut diagonally into ⅛-inch-thick slices
2 medium-size stalks celery, cut diagonally into ¼-inch-thick slices
1 can (8 oz.) water chestnuts, drained and thinly sliced
1 can (8 oz.) pineapple chunks in their own juice, drained
2 tablespoons cornstarch
½ cup firmly packed brown sugar
½ teaspoon minced fresh ginger or ¼ teaspoon ground ginger
¼ teaspoon crushed red pepper (optional)
2 tablespoons *each* soy sauce and dry sherry
½ cup *each* wine vinegar and regular-strength beef broth
1 to 1½ quarts shredded, lightly packed iceberg lettuce
1 can (5 oz.) chow mein noodles

Prepare Sesame Oven Meatballs as directed. In a large bowl, combine meatballs, green pepper, carrots, celery, water chestnuts, and pineapple; set aside.

In a small pan, combine cornstarch, brown sugar, ginger, red pepper (if desired), soy, sherry, vinegar, and broth; mix until smooth. Place over high heat and cook, stirring, until sauce boils and thickens. Pour over meatball mixture and stir gently to coat evenly.

Divide lettuce evenly among 4 to 6 dinner plates. Top lettuce with noodles; then spoon meatball mixture evenly over each serving. Makes 4 to 6 servings.

Sesame Oven Meatballs. In a bowl, combine ¼ cup *each* **fine dry bread crumbs** and finely chopped **green onions** (including tops), ½ cup **milk,** 1 **egg,** 1 clove **garlic** (minced or pressed), ½ teaspoon **salt,** ¼ teaspoon *each* **ground ginger** and **pepper,** 2 tablespoons **sesame seeds,** and 1 pound **lean ground beef.** Shape mixture into 1-inch balls and place on a rimmed baking sheet. Bake, uncovered, in a 500° oven for 10 to 12 minutes or until meat is no longer pink inside when slashed. Remove from pan with a slotted spatula and let drain on paper towels while continuing with recipe.

Steak & Vegetable Salad

An elegant but hearty meat salad

To complete the meal, we suggest crisp crackers and a light red wine.

1 flank steak (about 1½ lbs.) or 3½ cups thinly sliced cooked roast beef
2 tablespoons white wine vinegar
6 tablespoons salad oil
1 tablespoon Dijon mustard
½ teaspoon salt
¼ teaspoon pepper
1 pound small thin-skinned potatoes (about 2 inches in diameter)
½ pound green beans, ends removed
1 jar (6 oz.) marinated artichoke hearts, drained
1 can (7 oz.) whole pimentos, drained and cut into strips
¼ pound mushrooms, sliced
5 green onions (including tops), sliced

On a greased rack in a broiler pan, broil steak 4 inches below heat until browned on outside but still rare in center (about 5 minutes per side). Meanwhile, in a large bowl, combine vinegar, oil, mustard, salt, and pepper; blend with a wire whisk until well mixed.

Transfer steak to a carving board and cut across the grain into thin, slanting slices. Cut each slice into 2-inch lengths and add to mustard mixture; stir until steak is well coated with dressing.

Place potatoes in a medium-size pan; add water to cover. Place over high heat and bring to a boil; boil, covered, for 15 minutes. Add beans and continue to boil until potatoes are tender throughout when pierced and beans are just tender-crisp to bite (about 6 more minutes). Drain vegetables and rinse under cold running water until cool enough to handle; drain again. Peel potatoes, if desired, and cut into ¼-inch-thick slices; cut beans into 2-inch lengths. Add potatoes and beans to steak, along with artichoke hearts, pimentos, mushrooms, and onions. Toss until all ingredients are thoroughly coated with dressing. Serve at room temperature. Makes 6 or 7 servings.

It's the year of the quick meal, with Sesame Chicken Salad (page 20). This tempting Oriental version of chicken salad features crunchy Chinese pea pods and nutty toasted sesame seeds.

Quick Appetizer Ideas

Serve an appetizer before even the simplest meal—it adds sparkle to the menu, and needn't take long to prepare. This collection of easy appetizers provides a variety of choices, from simple dips and spreads to hot baked treats.

Dips

It's hard to resist dipping in, with homemade dips as good as these.

Quick Curry Dip

In a small bowl, stir together 1 cup **mayonnaise,** 1 tablespoon **curry powder** (or to taste), and 1 teaspoon **lemon juice** until well combined. Serve with crisp **raw vegetables** for dipping. Makes about 1 cup.

Guacamole

Cut 2 large ripe **avocados** in half, remove pits, and, with a spoon, scoop pulp into a bowl. With a fork, mash pulp coarsely while blending in 2 to 3 tablespoons **lime or lemon juice.** Add 1 clove **garlic** (minced or pressed) and 1 **tomato** (seeded and chopped); season to taste with **salt** and **liquid hot pepper seasoning.** Use **tortilla chips** or corn chips to scoop up dip. Makes about 2 cups.

Middle Eastern Hummus

Drain 1 can (15 oz.) **garbanzo beans,** reserving liquid. Place garbanzos in a blender or food processor, along with ¼ cup **tahini** (sesame paste), or ¼ cup toasted sesame seeds and 2 tablespoons olive oil. Add 3 tablespoons **lemon juice,** 1 large clove **garlic** (cut in thirds), ¼ cup of the reserved garbanzo liquid, ¼ teaspoon **ground cumin,** and ¼ teaspoon **ground red pepper** (cayenne). Whirl until mixture is smooth and the consistency of heavy batter, adding more garbanzo liquid if needed. Season to taste with **salt** and **pepper.** Garnish with **chopped parsley,** if desired, and scoop up with **pocket bread** (cut into quarters). Makes 1½ cups.

Spreads

For fanciers of full flavors, here are three creamy, cheesy spreads.

Brandied Blue Cheese Spread

In the small bowl of an electric mixer or in a food processor, place 3 ounces **blue-veined cheese,** 2 tablespoons **butter,** 1 small package (3 oz.) **cream cheese,** and 2 tablespoons **brandy.** Beat until smooth. Spread on red or golden Delicious **apple wedges** (coated with lemon juice to prevent browning), celery stalks, or unsalted crackers. Makes about 1 cup.

Smoked Salmon Spread

In the small bowl of an electric mixer or in a food processor, place 1 large package (8 oz.) **cream cheese,** 3 ounces **smoked salmon** (chopped), and 1 teaspoon **dill weed.** Beat until smooth. Spread on **cocktail-size bagels,** pumpernickel squares, or unsalted crackers. Makes about 1¼ cups.

Baked Camembert

Brush 1 **whole camembert cheese** (about 4 oz.) with **olive oil** on all sides; then roll in **fine dry bread crumbs** until completely coated. Place on an ovenproof plate or small baking dish and bake in a 350° oven for 12 to 15 minutes or until cheese just begins to melt. Spread on slices of **crusty bread** or crackers. Makes 3 or 4 servings.

Cold Meats

Dressed-up deli meats are a natural choice for speedy hors d'oeuvres.

Pastrami Roll-ups

In the small bowl of an electric mixer or in a food processor, place 1 small package (3 oz.) **cream cheese** and ¾ teaspoon **prepared horseradish.** Beat until smooth. Spread cream cheese mixture evenly on **pastrami slices** (you'll need about 4 oz. *total*); roll up jelly roll style. Cut into bite-size pieces, if desired. Makes 4 to 6 servings.

Easy Antipasto

On a platter, arrange 1 to 1½ pounds cold **Italian deli meats** (such as sliced dry salami, mortadella, zampino, galantina, coppa); 1 jar (6 oz.) **marinated artichoke hearts** (drained); and 1 jar (7½ oz.) **pickled Italian-style vegetables** (*giardiniera*), drained. Serve with **crusty bread** and **butter.** Makes 6 to 8 servings.

Baked Tidbits

Lend a party atmosphere to any meal with an appetizer hot from the oven.

Nachos

In a 9-inch square baking dish, arrange 4 cups **tortilla chips.** Sprinkle evenly with 1 cup (4 oz.) *each* shredded **jack** and **Cheddar cheese,** 2 tablespoons **diced green chiles,** and 2 tablespoons **sliced ripe olives.** Bake in a 350° oven for about 10 minutes or until cheese is melted. Top with a generous dollop of **sour cream** and serve immediately. Makes 4 servings.

Bacon-wrapped Dates

Cut 8 **bacon strips** in half crosswise; place on a rimmed baking sheet and broil 6 inches below heat until partially cooked but still soft (about 2½ minutes). Transfer to paper towels and let drain; discard excess fat from pan. Preheat oven to 400°. Place **pitted dates** at ends of bacon slices (1 date per slice) and roll up; place, seam side down, on baking sheet. Bake for 7 minutes or until bacon is crisp and dates are heated through. Serve warm. Makes 16.

Hasty Hots

In a small bowl, stir together 3 tablespoons **mayonnaise,** ¼ cup grated **Parmesan cheese,** and 2 **green onions** (including the tops), minced, until well combined. Broil about 12 slices **cocktail-size rye bread** about 6 inches below heat until toasted; turn over, spread cheese mixture on untoasted side, and broil until bubbly and lightly browned (about 3 minutes). Makes about 12.

Crunchy Nibbles

When you tire of ordinary crackers, substitute these special crunchy treats.

Won Ton Crispies

Melt 4 tablespoons **butter** or margarine in a small pan over medium heat. Brush some of the butter on a rimmed baking sheet. Cut 20 **won ton skins** in half, to make 40 rectangles; place as many skins on baking sheet as will fit without overlapping. Brush tops with butter; sprinkle with grated **Parmesan cheese** (you'll need about ½ cup *total*) and then with **instant minced onion,** if desired. Bake in a 375° oven for 5 to 6 minutes or until golden. Repeat until all are baked. Makes 40.

Garlic Toast

Thinly slice all or part of a **baguette** or loaf of other crusty bread; toast on both sides. Lightly rub a cut clove of **garlic** over one side of each hot slice; then brush on a liberal coating of **olive oil.** Sprinkle lightly with **pepper, oregano leaves,** and grated **Parmesan cheese.** Broil 6 inches from heat until cheese is lightly browned. Serve warm.

Chef's Salad

A big salad, full of crunch and color

To complete the meal, we suggest garlic bread and Chocolate Fondue (page 93).

1 cup Chili-spiced Thousand Island Dressing (page 20)
1 medium-size head iceberg lettuce, shredded
6 ounces cooked ham, cut into julienne strips (about 1 cup)
6 ounces Cheddar or jack cheese, cut into julienne strips (about 1½ cups)
½ cup sliced green onions (including tops)
1 basket cherry tomatoes, halved
2 hard-cooked eggs, chopped
1 can (3½ oz.) whole pitted ripe olives

Prepare Chili-spiced Thousand Island Dressing; cover and refrigerate.

Place lettuce in a large salad bowl. Arrange ham, cheese, onions, tomatoes, and eggs on top of lettuce in separate wedge-shaped sections; place olives in center.

Present salad at the table; just before serving, add dressing and toss gently. Makes 6 servings.

Fruit Salad Platter

Fresh fruit and ham dunked in yogurt dressing

Pictured on facing page

To complete the meal, we suggest warm buttered croissants and a cool beverage.

Hint for the cook: When summer fruits aren't available, substitute fresh fruits in season.

Orange-Yogurt Dressing (recipe follows)
1 basket strawberries, unhulled
1 small cantaloupe, seeds and rind removed, cut into 8 wedges
1 small pineapple, peeled, cored, and cut into spears
2 medium-size peaches or nectarines
Lemon juice
1 pound thinly sliced ham or turkey, or a combination
Orange zest (optional)

A colorful display of juicy summer fruits is the secret to **Fruit Salad Platter** (recipe on this page), a light and luscious entrée for brunch, lunch, or supper.

Prepare Orange-Yogurt Dressing; set aside. Just before serving, evenly divide strawberries, cantaloupe, and pineapple among 4 dinner plates. Peel peaches; pit and slice, then coat with lemon juice and divide among plates. Roll up ham slices and arrange next to fruit on each plate. Pour dressing evenly into 4 cups or small bowls, and place one on each plate; garnish with orange zest, if desired. At the table, dip fruit and ham into dressing as you eat. Makes 4 servings.

Orange-Yogurt Dressing. In a small bowl, stir together ¾ cup **plain yogurt,** ½ cup **sour cream,** 3 tablespoons **honey,** ½ teaspoon **grated orange peel,** and ¼ teaspoon **ground nutmeg.**

Italian-style Vermicelli Salad

Salami strips add zest to this garlicky pasta salad

To complete the meal, we suggest Italian bread sticks with butter, hot cooked green beans, and a hearty red wine.

1 package (8 oz.) vermicelli or spaghetti Boiling salted water
1 jar (6 oz.) marinated artichoke hearts
⅓ cup olive oil or salad oil
2 tablespoons white wine vinegar
1 teaspoon *each* oregano leaves and dry basil
¼ teaspoon *each* dry rosemary and pepper
2 cloves garlic, minced or pressed
1½ teaspoons dry mustard
1 medium-size carrot, finely diced
1 small zucchini, finely diced
1 package (3 oz.) sliced salami, cut into julienne strips
2 cups (8 oz.) shredded mozzarella cheese
⅓ cup grated Parmesan cheese
Lettuce leaves

Following package directions, cook vermicelli in a large kettle of boiling salted water until *al dente*; drain thoroughly, rinse with cold water, and drain again.

Drain marinade from artichoke hearts into a large bowl; chop hearts and set aside. To marinade, add oil, vinegar, oregano, basil, rosemary, pepper, garlic, mustard, and vermicelli. Stir to coat pasta thoroughly. Add carrot, zucchini, salami, mozzarella, Parmesan, and artichoke hearts. Stir well.

Line a platter with lettuce leaves and spoon pasta mixture into center. Serve at room temperature. Makes 6 servings.

Hearty Sandwiches

For greater efficiency:

Store bread in the freezer. You'll always have fresh bread for sandwiches if you keep it frozen. Bread kept at room temperature will become moldy if not used quickly, and refrigerated bread soon becomes stale, though it doesn't mold readily. To thaw frozen bread quickly, spread out slices in a single layer (in a warm place, if possible) and let stand for about 10 minutes; or if the bread is to be toasted, put slices directly into the toaster.

Make sandwiches ahead. For school lunches or other purposes, sandwiches can be made a day ahead and stored in the refrigerator. Spread the bread with butter to prevent sogginess; package lettuce and sliced tomato separately, to be added at the last minute. You can also freeze sandwiches for up to a week, but don't freeze those that contain mayonnaise or eggs—these ingredients do not freeze well.

Use your leftovers. Sandwiches are ideal vehicles for creative use of leftovers. Leftover meat loaf makes a delicious sandwich; so do cold cooked chicken, turkey, ham, beef, and lamb. Leftover fish can be combined with mayonnaise and seasonings to make a sandwich filling. And if you have a bit of sour cream or cream cheese to use up, or a creamy salad dressing such as Thousand Island (page 20), you can use it as a sandwich spread in place of the more common mayonnaise or butter.

Keep a supply of quick sandwich fixings. If you're really in a hurry and don't have time to follow a recipe, you can still make tempting sandwiches with ingredients from your pantry shelf or refrigerator. Keep on hand cans of tuna and boneless chicken; bacon and cold deli meats; hard-cooked eggs for egg salad; and a variety of cheeses and breads. Add lettuce, tomatoes, cucumbers, and/or alfalfa sprouts to sandwiches for juiciness, crunch, and color. And don't forget the peanut butter—it makes a good and nutritious sandwich filling combined with fruit, honey, bacon, or shredded lettuce, as well as partnered with the traditional jelly or jam.

Garden Vegetable Pockets

Vegetables and cheese tucked into pocket bread

To complete the meal, we suggest potato chips and ripe olives.

Hint for the cook: Other ingredients can be added to this sandwich filling—try ham, chicken, turkey, shrimp, crab, or hard-cooked eggs.

- 2 cups lightly packed shredded lettuce
- 1 cup shredded carrot
- 1 cup (4 oz.) shredded jack cheese
- ⅓ cup chopped green onions (including tops)
- 1 tomato, halved crosswise, seeded, and diced
- 1 avocado, pitted, peeled, and diced
- ¼ cup mayonnaise
- 3 tablespoons tomato-based chili sauce
- 1 tablespoon sweet pickle relish
- 3 pocket breads, halved

In a bowl, combine lettuce, carrot, cheese, onions, tomato, and avocado. In a cup, stir together mayonnaise, chili sauce, and relish; pour over vegetables and toss gently to blend. Fill pocket bread halves evenly with vegetable mixture, packing gently. Makes 3 to 6 servings.

Hot Crab Sandwiches

Creamy, delicate, and bubbling hot

To complete the meal, we suggest a spinach salad and Spiced Almonds & Melon (page 92).

- ½ pound cooked fresh or canned crabmeat
- 1 cup (4 oz.) shredded Swiss cheese
- 1 jar (2 oz.) diced pimentos, drained
- ⅓ cup *each* mayonnaise and finely chopped green pepper
- 4 slices firm-textured white bread
  Butter or margarine

In a bowl, combine crabmeat, cheese, pimentos, mayonnaise, and green pepper; stir until well blended. Meanwhile, toast bread. Spread each slice lightly with butter; then top evenly with crab mixture, spreading it out to edges. Place sandwiches on a baking sheet and broil 6 inches below heat until bubbly and heated through. Makes 4 servings.

Cheese & Chile Rolls

Hot, savory sandwiches for brunch, lunch, or supper

To complete the meal, we suggest a salad of crisp greens or fresh fruit.

- ¼ cup mayonnaise
- 2 tablespoons prepared mustard
- 1 teaspoon Worcestershire
- 1 can (7 oz.) diced green chiles, drained
- 1 can (4¼ oz.) chopped ripe olives, drained
- ½ cup thinly sliced green onions (including tops)
- 2 cups (8 oz.) shredded Cheddar cheese
- 3 French sandwich rolls, cut in half lengthwise
- 2 packages (4 oz. *each*) thinly sliced ham
- 2 medium-size tomatoes, thinly sliced

In a bowl, stir together mayonnaise, mustard, and Worcestershire. Stir in chiles, olives, onions, and cheese. Arrange roll halves, cut side up, on a rimmed baking sheet. Spoon cheese mixture evenly over each half. Arrange ham slices over cheese mixture, then top with tomato slices. Cover pan with foil; bake in a 400° oven for 20 to 25 minutes or until cheese is melted. Eat with knife and fork. Makes 6 servings.

Tuna Buns

A cheese-tuna combination that's great hot or cold

To complete the meal, we suggest cherry tomatoes and coleslaw.

- ⅔ cup mayonnaise
- 3 tablespoons sweet pickle relish
- 2 teaspoons prepared mustard
- 1 can (12½ oz.) chunk-style tuna, drained well and flaked
- 1 cup (4 oz.) shredded Cheddar cheese
- ½ cup *each* chopped celery and green onions (including tops)
- 4 onion or kaiser-style rolls

In a bowl, stir together mayonnaise, relish, and mustard. Add tuna, cheese, celery, and onions; stir until well combined. Spread tuna mixture evenly over bottom halves of rolls; top with remaining roll halves. Makes 4 servings.

To serve hot: Wrap each sandwich in foil. Place on a baking sheet in a 350° oven for 15 to 20 minutes or until cheese is melted. Unwrap and serve immediately.

Shrimp Stack Sandwiches

Cool and dill-seasoned; eat with a knife and fork

Pictured on facing page

To complete the meal, we suggest potato chips, a cup of soup, and cold beer; serve butter cookies for dessert.

> ¼ cup *each* mayonnaise and sour cream
> 1 teaspoon *each* lemon juice and dill weed
> ½ teaspoon prepared horseradish
> 4 slices firm-textured white or wheat bread
> 1 large tomato, thinly sliced
> 1 pound small cooked shrimp
> 1 avocado, pitted, peeled, and thinly sliced
> Dill sprigs and lemon wedges (optional)

In a small bowl, place mayonnaise, sour cream, lemon juice, dill weed, and horseradish; stir until smooth. Spread a little of the dill mixture over each bread slice; top with a few tomato slices. Evenly distribute shrimp atop tomato slices; spoon remaining dill mixture over shrimp. Top sandwiches with avocado slices. Garnish with dill sprigs and lemon wedges, if desired. Makes 4 servings.

Chicken-Artichoke Monte Cristos

Satisfying French-toasted sandwiches

To complete the meal, we suggest a crisp green salad, iced tea, and Pineapple with Sour Cream Topping (page 92).

> 1½ cups shredded cooked chicken
> 1 jar (6 oz.) marinated artichoke hearts, drained well and chopped
> 1 tablespoon *each* mayonnaise and dry sherry
> ¾ teaspoon dry rosemary
> 8 slices firm-textured white bread
> 4 square slices (4 oz. *total*) Swiss or jack cheese
> 2 eggs
> ¼ cup milk
> About 2 tablespoons butter or margarine

In a bowl, stir together chicken, artichoke hearts, mayonnaise, sherry, and rosemary until well combined. Spread chicken mixture evenly over 4 of the bread slices, top each with a slice of cheese, then with one of the remaining 4 slices of bread, pressing lightly to hold the sandwiches together.

In a pie pan, beat together eggs and milk until well blended. Melt about 1 tablespoon of the butter in a wide frying pan over medium heat. Meanwhile, dip 2 of the sandwiches in egg mixture to coat both sides; drain briefly. Place in frying pan, cheese side down; cook, turning once, until golden brown on both sides (about 5 minutes *total*). Remove from pan and keep warm. Repeat with remaining 2 sandwiches, adding more butter as needed. Serve immediately; eat with knife and fork. Makes 4 servings.

Turkey & Bacon Salad Sandwiches

A cross between a salad and a sandwich

To complete the meal, we suggest a cool beverage and Cream Sundaes (page 92).

> 8 slices firm-textured white, wheat, or rye bread
> Butter, margarine, or mayonnaise
> 1 quart lightly packed shredded lettuce
> ¼ cup sliced green onions (including tops)
> 1 pound thinly sliced cooked turkey
> ¼ cup sliced radishes
> 12 strips bacon, crisply cooked and drained
> 1 avocado, pitted, peeled, and sliced
> Salt and pepper
> Cherry tomatoes
> Chili-spiced Thousand Island Dressing (page 20) or Green Goddess Dressing

Toast both sides of bread slices; spread one side of each slice with butter. Place 2 slices side by side on each of 4 salad plates, butter side up; cover evenly with lettuce and sprinkle with onions. Evenly distribute turkey, radishes, bacon, and avocado atop lettuce. Season with salt and pepper, and garnish with cherry tomatoes. At the table, pass dressing to spoon over top; eat with knife and fork. Makes 4 servings.

Spilling over the sides of this open-faced entrée is an ocean of succulent small shrimp. Along with chips, hot soup, and a tall glass of beer, Shrimp Stack Sandwiches (recipe on this page) make a satisfying meal.

Italian Sausage & Pepper Sandwiches

Juicy sausages in a rich, tomatoey sauce

To complete the meal, we suggest red wine and a tossed green salad.

>   4 mild Italian sausages (1 to 1½ lbs. *total*)
>   2 tablespoons olive oil or salad oil
>   1 large onion, thinly sliced and separated into rings
>   1 clove garlic, minced or pressed
>   3 medium-size green or red bell peppers, seeded and cut into thin strips
>   1 can (15 oz.) Italian-style tomatoes
>   1 tablespoon *each* dry basil and sugar
>   Salt and pepper
>   4 French rolls or hot dog buns

In a wide frying pan over medium heat, cook sausages until well browned; remove from pan and set aside. Add oil, onion, garlic, and peppers to drippings; cook, stirring occasionally, until vegetables are soft (about 15 minutes).

Stir in tomatoes (break up with a spoon) and their liquid, basil, and sugar. Add sausages and cook, covered, for 15 minutes. Uncover, increase heat to medium-high, and cook, stirring occasionally, until almost all liquid has evaporated (about 5 minutes). Season to taste with salt and pepper. Place a sausage in each roll and spoon some sauce over top; close and eat out of hand. Or leave open-faced and eat with knife and fork. Makes 4 servings.

Pineapple Pork Burgers

Out-of-the-ordinary open-faced burgers

To complete the meal, we suggest carrot sticks and fruit sherbet.

>   1 pound lean ground pork
>   1 egg
>   1 clove garlic, minced or pressed
>   1 medium-size onion, finely chopped
>   ½ medium-size green pepper, seeded and finely chopped
>   ½ teaspoon *each* salt and ground cumin
>   ¼ teaspoon *each* pepper and oregano leaves
>   2 English muffins, split and toasted
>   1 can (8 oz.) pineapple slices in their own juice (4 slices), drained

In a bowl, stir together pork, egg, garlic, onion, green pepper, salt, cumin, pepper, and oregano until well combined. Divide into 4 equal portions and shape each into a patty about 4 inches in diameter. Cook patties in a wide frying pan over medium heat until well browned and no longer pink inside when slashed (6 to 7 minutes per side).

Remove patties from pan; place on muffin halves on a baking sheet and keep warm in a 200° oven. Add pineapple slices to pan and cook, turning once, until lightly browned on both sides. Top each burger with a pineapple slice; eat with knife and fork. Makes 4 servings.

Giant Sesame Ham Sandwich

A sandwich made from a hollowed-out loaf of bread

To complete the meal, we suggest iced tea, fruit, and cookies.

>   6 tablespoons salad oil
>   2 tablespoons sesame seeds
>   1 teaspoon ground ginger
>   3 tablespoons white wine vinegar
>   1½ tablespoons soy sauce
>   1 teaspoon sugar
>   1 clove garlic, minced or pressed
>   ½ cup sliced green onions (including tops)
>   ½ pound cooked ham, cut into julienne strips (about 1½ cups)
>   1 can (8 oz.) water chestnuts, drained and thinly sliced
>   1 package (6 oz.) frozen Chinese pea pods, thawed and drained
>   1 cup thinly sliced celery
>   ⅓ pound mushrooms, thinly sliced
>   1 round loaf crusty bread (24 oz.) or 2 oblong loaves (1 lb. *each*)

In a frying pan over medium-low heat, combine oil and sesame seeds; cook, stirring, until seeds are golden (2 to 4 minutes). Let cool; then stir in ginger, vinegar, soy, sugar, garlic, and onions.

In a bowl, stir together ham, water chestnuts, pea pods, celery, and mushrooms. Reserve 1 to 2 tablespoons sesame dressing; add the rest to ham mixture.

Slice off top portion of bread loaf to form a ½ to ¾-inch-thick lid. Pull out soft center of bread, leaving a shell about ⅜ inch thick (reserve soft bread for other uses). Spoon ham mixture into bread bowl; drizzle reserved sesame dressing over cut side of lid; place on top. To serve, cut into wedges. Makes 6 servings.

Timesaver: The Microwave Oven

Microwaving is a boon to the busy cook. Even if you don't want to prepare a whole meal in it, you can save a lot of time by using the microwave for small tasks. Here we give you a miscellany of microwave tips to help you speed up your food preparation.

Reheating bread products

The microwave reheats baked breads, sweet rolls, and doughnuts easily and quickly—so quickly, in fact, that you'll need to be very vigilant. It takes just 10 to 15 seconds on high (100%) to reheat each roll or bread slice.

To reheat a roll or bread slice, wrap it in a paper towel or paper napkin (to prevent a soggy bottom); then heat only until the outside feels warm to the touch. If heated too long, it will become tough and hard when cool.

In sweet rolls, the sugary fillings and icings attract more microwaves than the pastry or bread itself, so to avoid burning yourself, allow a few minutes standing time.

Melting a stick of butter or margarine

Unwrap 1 stick (½ cup) butter and place it in a 10-ounce dish or custard cup. Microwave, uncovered, on high (100%) for 1 minute.

Softening a stick of butter or margarine

Unwrap 1 stick (½ cup) butter and place it on a saucer. Microwave, uncovered, on medium (50%) for 10 to 15 seconds. Let stand for 5 minutes to complete softening.

Softening cream cheese

Unwrap a package of cream cheese and place it on a small plate; cover with wax paper. Microwave a small package (3 oz.) on medium (50%) for 30 seconds to 1 minute. Microwave a large package (8 oz.) for 1½ to 2 minutes.

Softening refrigerated cheese

For easier slicing of refrigerated cheese, wrap it in plastic wrap and place directly on floor of microwave. (Or put cheese on a plate and cover loosely with plastic wrap.) Microwave on medium (50%) for 30 seconds to 1 minute (depending on size) or until cheese is slightly soft to the touch.

Softening ice cream for easier serving

Place unopened ½ gallon hard ice cream on oven floor. Microwave on medium (50%) for 45 seconds to 1 minute; let stand for a minute or two before serving.

Warming tortillas and crêpes

To warm an unopened package of tortillas, cut a slit in package and place it on oven floor. Microwave on high (100%) for 1 minute. Or wrap the number of tortillas or crêpes you need in paper towels; microwave on high (100%) for 6 to 7 seconds per piece.

To soften frozen juice concentrates

Remove one end of a 6 or 12-oz. can of frozen juice. Place, upright, directly on oven floor. Microwave on high (100%) for 1 minute. Let concentrate stand for a minute or two before preparing.

To make regular-strength broth

Drop a bouillon cube (chicken or beef) or a teaspoon of stock base in a 1-cup glass measure filled with tap water. Microwave, uncovered, on high (100%) for 1½ to 2 minutes. Stir until bouillon has dissolved.

Spicy Beef Burritos

Dinner wrapped up in a soft flour tortilla

Pictured on facing page

To complete the meal, we suggest sangría and fresh fruit of the season.

Hints for the cook: To keep meat juicy and tender, stir-fry only briefly. If overcooked, it will toughen. To warm tortillas in a microwave, see page 33.

> **Condiments:** Shredded lettuce, diced tomatoes, shredded Cheddar or jack cheese, sour cream, sliced avocado (coated with lemon juice to prevent browning), cilantro sprigs, and taco sauce
>
> 6 large flour tortillas (*each* about 10 inches in diameter)
> ¼ cup salad oil
> 2 pounds boneless top round steak (about 1 inch thick), thinly sliced across the grain, then cut into 2-inch-long strips
> 1 large onion, chopped
> 2 cloves garlic, minced or pressed
> 1½ teaspoons *each* ground cumin and chili powder
> ¼ teaspoon oregano leaves
> ⅛ teaspoon ground red pepper (cayenne)
> Salt

Prepare condiments and place on a platter or in individual bowls. Stack tortillas, wrap in foil, and place in a 350° oven for 15 minutes or until heated through.

Meanwhile, heat 2 tablespoons of the oil in a wide frying pan over medium-high heat. Add half the meat and stir-fry until meat is brown on the outside but still pink within (about 5 minutes); remove from pan. Repeat with remaining 2 tablespoons oil and remaining meat. To drippings, add onion, garlic, cumin, chili powder, oregano, and red pepper. Reduce heat to medium and cook, stirring, until onion is soft (10 to 15 minutes). Add meat; stir until well combined and cook just until heated through. Season to taste with salt.

To eat, spoon filling onto a warm tortilla, top with condiments, and roll up. Makes 6 servings.

Fix a no-fuss fiesta with Spicy Beef Burritos (recipe on this page)—they're do-it-yourself sandwiches made from a zesty, Mexican-seasoned beef mixture and your choice of colorful condiments all wrapped up in warm flour tortillas to eat out of your hand.

Armenian Tortilla Pizzas

A Mexican crust with an Armenian topping

To complete the meal, we suggest a selection of finger vegetables, and cookies and fruit.

> 1 pound lean ground lamb
> 1 cup finely chopped green or red bell pepper, or a combination
> 2 large cloves garlic, minced or pressed
> ½ cup chopped parsley
> 3 tablespoons tomato paste
> 1 can (15 oz.) Italian-style tomatoes
> 1 teaspoon *each* paprika and ground allspice
> ¼ teaspoon pepper
> Salt
> 6 flour tortillas (*each* 7 to 8 inches in diameter)
> 1¼ cups (5 oz.) shredded mozzarella cheese

Crumble lamb into a wide frying pan over medium-high heat. Add green pepper and garlic and cook, stirring often, until meat is browned (5 to 7 minutes); spoon off and discard excess fat. Stir in parsley, tomato paste, tomatoes (break up with a spoon) and their liquid, paprika, allspice, and pepper. Reduce heat and simmer, uncovered, until liquid has evaporated (about 10 minutes). Season to taste with salt.

Place 3 of the tortillas on a large baking sheet. Spoon about ½ cup of the meat mixture over each tortilla; spread out to within ¼ inch of edges. Sprinkle with some of the cheese; broil about 6 inches below heat until cheese is melted. Repeat with remaining 3 tortillas, meat mixture, and cheese. Eat out of hand or with knife and fork. Makes 6 servings.

Italian Tortilla Pizzas

Prepare **Armenian Tortilla Pizzas,** but substitute 1 pound **lean ground beef** for the lamb, omit paprika and allspice, and add 1 teaspoon **Italian herb seasoning** (or ¼ teaspoon *each* dry basil and oregano, thyme, and marjoram leaves).

Mexican Tortilla Pizzas

Prepare **Armenian Tortilla Pizzas,** but substitute ½ pound **lean ground beef** and ½ pound **chorizo sausage** (casings removed), or 1 pound lean ground beef for the lamb. Omit paprika and allspice, and add 1 teaspoon **chili powder** and ½ teaspoon *each* **ground cumin** and **oregano leaves.**

Eggs & Cheese

For greater efficiency:

Know your eggs and how to use them. Keep eggs in the refrigerator, covered to prevent absorption of odors. Stored in this way, they'll keep for as long as a month. But you'll have best results if you use your freshest eggs for poaching or frying; use others for hard-cooking, scrambling, or in recipes requiring beaten eggs. If you need beaten whites, bring the eggs to room temperature by immersing them in hot tap water for a minute or two, then separate them—they'll whip up to greater volume.

Save unused egg. If a recipe calls for egg whites only, you can store the yolks in the refrigerator for as long as 2 days. Place yolks in a small bowl, add just enough cold water to cover them with a thin film, and cover the bowl airtight with plastic wrap. Use the yolks to enrich sauces or scrambled eggs; measure out 1 tablespoon for each large egg yolk needed. If you're saving whites, store them in a jar with a screw-on lid; measure out 2 tablespoons for each egg white needed.

If you halve a recipe and find you need only half an egg, beat a whole one, then measure out half of it (about 1½ tablespoons). Reserve the remaining egg for other uses; you can store it in the refrigerator, covered, for up to 2 days.

Never rush egg and cheese dishes. Eggs are delicate and must be cooked gently to avoid rubbery results; cheese, too, becomes tough and stringy when exposed to high or prolonged temperatures during cooking.

Store cheese properly. To avoid waste, wrap cheese tightly in plastic wrap and keep in the refrigerator—many varieties keep for several weeks. If surface mold spots develop, they can be cut off and discarded; the rest of the cheese won't be affected.

Keep shredded cheese on hand. Consider what types of shredded cheese you use most, and try shredding some ahead of time and keeping it refrigerated in a plastic bag or tightly covered container to save time during meal preparation. A food processor can make cheese-grating much faster—and easier on the knuckles (see page 15).

Eggs & Asparagus Milanese

A springtime treat of Italian origin

To complete the meal, we suggest crusty rolls, chilled white wine, and almond macaroons.

> 12 to 16 asparagus spears
> 4 tablespoons butter or margarine
> 8 to 12 eggs
> ½ cup freshly shredded Parmesan cheese
> Coarsely ground pepper

Preheat oven to 450°. Remove tough ends of asparagus; rinse well. Add 1 inch water to a wide frying pan and bring to a boil over high heat; add asparagus to pan in a single layer. When water resumes a full rolling boil, cover and boil just until asparagus is tender-crisp (7 to 10 minutes).

Meanwhile, place 1 tablespoon of the butter in each of four shallow 7-inch oval or 6-inch round baking dishes. Set dishes on a baking sheet in oven for about 5 minutes or until butter is melted.

Remove baking sheet from oven and quickly place 3 or 4 asparagus spears in each dish; push to one side. Carefully break 2 or 3 eggs side by side into each dish; immediately return sheet to oven and bake until eggs are set to your liking (yolks will be soft-cooked after 5 to 7 minutes). Sprinkle cheese evenly over eggs; bake for about 1 more minute or until cheese is melted. Sprinkle each serving with pepper. Makes 4 servings.

Rocky Mountain Eggs

A sturdy egg-and-potato entrée for two

To complete the meal, we suggest a crisp green salad and Broiled Tomatoes Parmesan (page 53).

> 4 tablespoons butter or margarine
> 1 or 2 small thin-skinned potatoes, peeled and cut into ½-inch cubes (about ¾ cup)
> 1 small onion, finely chopped
> ½ cup diced cooked ham, beef, or pork
> 1 tablespoon chopped parsley
> 3 eggs
> ¼ teaspoon salt
> Dash of pepper
> 1 tablespoon milk
> ½ cup shredded Cheddar or jack cheese

In a 10-inch frying pan over medium heat, melt 2 tablespoons of the butter. Add potatoes, onion,

and ham; cover and cook, stirring occasionally, until potatoes are tender when pierced (about 15 minutes). Sprinkle with parsley, add remaining butter, and distribute mixture evenly in pan.

In a bowl, beat eggs with salt, pepper, and milk until well blended. Pour egg mixture into pan and cook without stirring. As egg mixture begins to set, lift edges with a spatula and tilt pan to let uncooked egg flow underneath. Continue cooking until eggs are softly set; top should still be moist. Remove from heat and sprinkle with cheese; cover pan just until cheese is melted. Cut into wedges to serve. Makes 2 servings.

Egg Foo Yung

Fried Chinese egg patties, crunchy with sprouts

To complete the meal, we suggest steamed rice and fresh fruit of the season.

> ¾ cup regular-strength chicken broth
> 2 tablespoons soy sauce
> ½ teaspoon ground ginger
> ¼ teaspoon *each* liquid hot pepper seasoning and garlic powder
> 1 tablespoon cornstarch
> ⅓ cup water
> 6 eggs
> 1½ cups diced cooked pork or ham
> ⅔ cup thinly sliced green onions (including tops)
> ¼ pound bean sprouts, coarsely chopped
> About 4 tablespoons salad oil
> ¼ pound mushrooms, coarsely chopped

In a 1 to 2-quart pan combine broth, soy, ginger, hot pepper seasoning, garlic powder, cornstarch, and water; stir until blended. Cook over medium-high heat, stirring constantly, until bubbly and thickened. Cover and keep hot.

In a bowl, beat eggs until blended; stir in pork, onions, and bean sprouts. In a wide frying pan, heat 2 tablespoons of the oil over medium-high heat; add mushrooms and cook, stirring occasionally, until liquid has evaporated. Lift out with a slotted spoon and add to egg mixture.

Heat 2 more tablespoons oil in pan over medium-high heat. When oil is hot, pour egg mixture into pan in ¼-cup portions; shape each portion into a patty (you can cook 3 or 4 at a time). Cook patties, turning once, until golden on both sides (about 3 minutes *total*); remove from pan and keep warm. Repeat until all egg mixture is used, adding more oil as needed. Pour hot sauce over patties and serve at once. Makes 4 servings.

Olive & Artichoke Soufflé

For an elegant brunch, lunch, or supper

To complete the meal, we suggest croissants and a crunchy stir-fried vegetable mélange.

Hint for the cook: For a more substantial meal, serve the soufflé as a side dish to accompany simple grilled or pan-broiled meats.

> Grated Parmesan cheese
> 1 jar (6 oz.) marinated artichoke hearts
> 1 cup milk
> ¼ cup butter or margarine
> ¼ cup all-purpose flour
> ½ teaspoon salt
> 1½ cups (6 oz.) shredded jack cheese
> 1 can (2¼ oz.) sliced ripe olives, drained
> 6 eggs, separated
> ¼ teaspoon cream of tartar

Preheat oven to 450°. Thoroughly grease a 2 to 2½-quart soufflé dish; then dust bottom and sides with Parmesan cheese. Set aside. Drain artichokes; add 2 tablespoons of the marinade to milk and set aside (discard any remaining marinade, or use for other purposes). Chop artichokes coarsely and set aside.

In a 2-quart pan over medium heat, melt butter. Add flour and cook, stirring, until bubbles form around edges of pan; continue to cook and stir for 1 minute (mixture should bubble continuously). Remove from heat. Stirring constantly with a wire whisk, gradually add milk mixture. Return to heat and cook, stirring constantly, until mixture boils and thickens. Stir in salt, jack cheese, olives, and artichokes; remove from heat.

With a spoon, lightly beat egg yolks. Spoon about 2 tablespoons of the sauce into yolks and stir until all sauce has been incorporated; then stir egg yolk mixture back into sauce in pan, blending thoroughly.

Beat egg whites until frothy. Add cream of tartar and beat until soft, moist peaks form. Fold about ⅓ of beaten whites into sauce mixture; then add sauce to egg whites by carefully pouring sauce into space left when first ⅓ of egg whites was removed. Gently fold sauce and whites together.

Pour into prepared dish. Bake for 12 minutes at 450°, then reduce oven temperature to 250° and bake for 20 more minutes or until top is golden and center jiggles only slightly when dish is gently shaken (test quickly and close oven door promptly). Serve immediately. Makes 4 to 6 servings.

Individual Omelet

A quick and versatile entrée for any occasion

Pictured on facing page

To complete the meal, we suggest browned sausages, bagels, and a crisp salad or fresh fruit.

Hint for the cook: If you plan to use a filling, have it ready and nearby before you begin cooking.

> 2 or 3 eggs
> ¼ teaspoon salt
> Dash of pepper
> 1 tablespoon water
> 3 teaspoons butter or margarine
> Omelet fillings (optional; suggestions follow)

Break eggs into a small bowl and add salt, pepper, and water. Beat with a fork just enough to mix yolks and whites.

In a 7 to 8-inch omelet pan with a nonstick finish, over medium-high heat, melt 1½ teaspoons of the butter and heat until foam begins to subside. Pour in egg mixture all at once. As edges begin to set (this will happen almost at once), lift with a spatula and shake or tilt pan to let uncooked egg flow underneath. When egg no longer flows freely, spoon one or a combination of fillings on one half of omelet, if desired. Run a spatula around edge, fold omelet in half, and slide onto a warm plate. Spread remaining 1½ teaspoons butter over top of omelet. Makes 1 serving.

Savory omelet fillings. Shredded **cheese** (jack, Cheddar, or Parmesan); diced **avocado; alfalfa sprouts;** sliced **mushrooms** (raw or sautéed in butter); cooked crumbled **bacon;** thinly sliced **ham; salami** slivers; small cooked **shrimp** (or flaked crab or tuna); **salted sunflower seeds;** diced **tomatoes.**

Sweet omelet fillings. Sliced **peaches, nectarines, bananas,** or **apricots** (sprinkled with lemon juice); sliced **strawberries; kiwi** rounds; shredded **coconut;** chopped **nuts; sour cream; brown sugar.**

Whether you've having a party or dining in solitary splendor, the Individual Omelet (recipe on this page) is an ideal quick-meal choice. Filled with fresh fruit, nuts, and brown sugar, it makes a marvelous brunch.

Quick Breakfast Ideas

Even on busy mornings, it's possible to put together an appealing and nutritious breakfast in just a few minutes. Eggs, of course, are the traditional fare when time is short—cooked in any number of ways, they make an excellent quick breakfast.

But how many cooks have ventured past the reliable egg to try the idea of breakfast in a glass? Or in a soup bowl? Or served up as a hearty sandwich? Following is a collection of creative recipes that are sure to start your day off right. They're delicious and protein-packed—and best of all, they won't take all morning to prepare.

Breakfast drinks

Get some nutrition into those who think they don't like breakfast! These soothing beverages go down easily even at an early hour. Two are savory hot drinks; the others are cool, creamy, milkshake-like creations. Serve with buttered toast, if you like.

Hot Milk Broth

In a small pan over medium-high heat, combine 2 cups **milk,** 1 teaspoon **butter** or margarine (optional), and 2 teaspoons **chicken or beef stock base** (or 2 chicken or beef bouillon cubes, crumbled). Heat just to simmering, stirring often; do not boil. In a blender, whirl 2 to 4 **eggs** until frothy; with motor running, gradually add hot milk mixture to eggs. Pour into 2 large glasses or mugs; top with a dash of **pepper** (optional) and grated **Parmesan cheese.** Makes 2 servings.

Hot Breakfast Broth

Follow directions for **Hot Milk Broth,** substituting 2 cups regular-strength **chicken or beef broth** for the milk, butter, and stock base. Makes 2 servings.

Strawberry Nog

In a blender, whirl until smooth: 2½ cups sliced **strawberries,** 1 can (6 oz.) **frozen orange juice concentrate** (undiluted), 1½ cups **milk,** 1 cup **ice cubes,** ¼ cup **sugar,** 1 teaspoon **vanilla,** and **2 eggs.** Makes 4 to 6 servings.

Orange & Banana Cream

In a blender, whirl until smooth: 2 ripe **bananas** (peeled and cut into chunks), **2 eggs,** 1⅓ cups **orange juice,** and 1 cup **vanilla ice cream.** Makes 2 servings.

Blueberry-Lemon Smoothee

In a blender, whirl until smooth: 1 cup fresh or frozen **blueberries,** 1 cup **lemon-flavored yogurt,** 2 tablespoons **brown sugar,** 1 tablespoon **lemon juice,** and ½ cup **ice cubes.** Makes 2 servings.

Golden Fruit Whirl

In a blender, whirl until smooth: 1 cup drained canned **apricot halves** or sliced peaches (or partially thawed, frozen, sweetened peaches), 1 cup **plain yogurt,** ¾ cup **orange juice,** and 3 tablespoons **honey.** Makes 3 or 4 servings.

Soups

A perfect choice for a winter morning, these fortifying bowlfuls will make you wonder why you never thought of eating soup for breakfast before. The clam broth is a light soup, the chowder thick and rich.

Clam Broth

In a small pan over medium heat, melt 1 tablespoon **butter** or margarine; add 1 **green onion** (including top), thinly sliced, and cook until soft (about 1 minute). Drain juice from 1 can (6½ oz.) **minced clams** into pan; add 2 cups **milk,** ¼ teaspoon **white pepper,** and ⅛ teaspoon **thyme leaves.** Increase heat to medium-high and heat broth until steaming. Add clams and cook, stirring, just until heated through (about 1 minute). Serve immediately in bowls or mugs. Makes 2 servings.

Corn & Sausage Chowder

In a small pan over medium heat, melt 1 tablespoon **butter** or margarine. Add 1 **kielbasa** (Polish sausage), thinly sliced, and cook, stirring, until browned (about 3 minutes). Spoon off and discard fat; stir in 1 can (about 17 oz.) **cream-style corn,** ½ to ¾ cup **milk,** ½ teaspoon **chili powder,** and ⅛ teaspoon **ground cumin.** Heat until steaming. Makes 2 servings.

Sandwiches

Sandwiches are an ingenious way of getting a good, solid breakfast into a neat little package that's easy to make and eat. The following recipes show how versatile the breakfast sandwich can be; you might also try experimenting with your own ideas, using any combination of ingredients that appeals to you.

Breakfast Ham & Cheese Sandwiches

In the small bowl of an electric mixer or in a food processor, place 1 tablespoon chopped **Major Grey chutney** and 1 small package (3 oz.) **cream cheese;** beat just until well combined. Spread about 2 teaspoons cream cheese mixture on each of 8 slices **white or wheat bread** (toasted, if desired). Evenly distribute 1 package (4 oz.) **sliced ham** atop 4 slices of the bread; top with remaining 4 slices. Makes 4 servings.

Quesadillas

Preheat oven to 450°. Cover half of 1 **flour tortilla** (about 8 inches in diameter) with ½ cup shredded **cheese** (Cheddar, jack, Swiss, American, or teleme) to within ½ inch of edge. Sprinkle with 1 tablespoon chopped, seeded canned **green chile** (optional). Fold uncovered half of tortilla over cheese; place on a baking sheet in oven for 5 minutes or until cheese is melted and tortilla is lightly browned. Serve immediately. Makes 1 serving.

Note: for spicier quesadillas, drizzle 1 tablespoon taco sauce over cheese before folding; or, for meat filling, use only ¼ cup cheese and add 1 slice (or about ¼ cup diced) cooked chicken, turkey, or beef.

Strawberry Sandwiches

Toast 2 slices **raisin bread** and spread with **butter** or margarine. Cover each with small whole **strawberries,** hulled side down. Sprinkle evenly with shredded **jack cheese;** broil about 6 inches below heat just until cheese is melted. Makes 2 servings.

Ricotta-Fruit Muffins

In a bowl, stir together 1 cup (8 oz.) **ricotta cheese,** 2 to 3 tablespoons **honey,** 2 teaspoons **lemon juice,** and ½ teaspoon **ground cinnamon** until well combined. Spread equal amounts of cheese mixture over 4 **toasted and buttered English muffin halves.** Top with **berries,** sliced peaches, or other fruit of your choice. Makes 2 to 4 servings.

Peanut Butter & Banana Sandwiches

Toast 4 slices **whole wheat bread;** while hot, spread 2 of the slices with chunk-style **peanut butter** and top with 1 **banana,** sliced, dividing fruit evenly. Spread remaining 2 slices bread generously with **honey** and place over bananas, honey side down. Makes 2 servings.

Chiles Rellenos Casserole

Puffy golden dome conceals chiles and cheese

To complete the meal, we suggest refried beans and a salad of iceberg lettuce, avocado, and tomato.

    1 can (4 oz.) whole green chiles, split lengthwise and seeded
    4 ounces jack cheese, sliced ¼ inch thick
    3 eggs, separated

In a greased 8-inch square baking dish, lay chiles out flat; cover evenly with cheese slices. In a bowl, beat egg whites until stiff, moist peaks form. In another bowl, beat yolks until well combined. Fold beaten yolks gently into whites and spoon evenly over cheese.

Bake, uncovered, in a 350° oven for 20 minutes or until egg is lightly browned. Serve immediately. Makes 3 or 4 servings.

Crustless Zucchini Quiche

Instead of a crust, a layer of wheat germ

To complete the meal, we suggest chewy whole-grain bread and a fruit salad.

Hint for the cook: Handle the zucchini shreds as little as possible; handling makes them watery.

    1 tablespoon butter or margarine
    ¼ cup regular wheat germ
    ½ cup shredded Swiss cheese
    ¼ cup chopped green onions (including tops)
    2 small zucchini (about ½ lb. *total*), coarsely shredded
    1 cup (4 oz.) shredded jack cheese
    8 eggs
    ¼ cup milk
    2 cloves garlic, minced or pressed
    ¼ teaspoon salt
    ¾ teaspoon pepper
    ¼ cup grated Parmesan cheese

The Swiss invented fondue, but they might not recognize this one! Chunky Cheddar Fondue (recipe on this page) is lively in flavor and boasts a variety of distinctive dippers.

Spread butter generously over bottom and up sides of a 9-inch pie pan; evenly sprinkle with wheat germ. Top with an even layer of Swiss cheese, then onions, then zucchini. Sprinkle with jack cheese; set aside.

In a bowl, beat eggs and milk until blended. Stir in garlic, salt, pepper, and Parmesan cheese; pour egg mixture over jack cheese in pie pan.

Bake, uncovered, in a 350° oven for 25 to 30 minutes or until a knife inserted in center comes out clean. Let stand for 10 minutes before cutting into wedges. Makes 6 servings.

Chunky Cheddar Fondue

Bubbly cheese laced with chile and tomato bits

Pictured on facing page

To complete the meal, we suggest wine or a cold beverage, and Berry Slush (page 93).

Hint for the cook: If fondue begins to cool, reheat it over medium heat, stirring occasionally, until cheese is melted. Or microwave in a glass or ceramic container on medium (50%) for 1 minute (stir after 30 seconds) or until heated through.

    Assorted raw vegetables: Green pepper strips, carrot sticks or whole baby carrots, zucchini rounds, celery sticks, mushrooms (quartered if large), green onions, cauliflower florets
    Firm French bread cubes, tortilla chips, or bread sticks
    3 tablespoons butter or margarine
    1 medium-size onion, chopped
    1 small can (about 8 oz.) stewed tomatoes
    1 can (4 oz.) whole green chiles, seeded and chopped
    ¼ teaspoon oregano leaves
    4 cups (1 lb.) shredded Cheddar cheese

Prepare vegetables and bread; set aside. In a 10-inch frying pan over medium heat, melt butter. Add onion and cook, stirring occasionally, until lightly browned (about 10 minutes). Stir in tomatoes (break up with a spoon) and their liquid, chiles, and oregano. Reduce heat and simmer, uncovered, for 5 minutes. Add cheese, a handful at a time, stirring until cheese is melted and mixture is well blended.

If desired, transfer to a fondue pot or chafing dish and keep warm over heat source. If serving in frying pan, reheat as necessary (see "Hint for the cook"). Use assorted vegetables and bread cubes as dippers. Makes about 3 cups (3 or 4 servings).

Pasta & Grains

For greater efficiency:

Start pasta water boiling first. It takes time for a large quantity of water to boil, so get it started before continuing with the recipe. Then it will be boiling when you need to cook your pasta; if it comes to a rolling boil before you're ready, turn the heat down to simmer. Just before you want to cook, increase the heat again, and the water will boil fairly rapidly.

Cook pasta correctly. Use 3 quarts water and 1 tablespoon salt for 8 ounces (½ lb.) packaged dried pasta. To cook a pound of dried pasta, double the water only. After adding pasta to boiling water, boil uncovered and start timing after water resumes a full rolling boil. Start taste-testing before the time recommended on the package is up. Pasta should be *al dente*—literally, "to the tooth," or tender to bite but still firm; the same is true for rice. Have a colander waiting in the sink to drain pasta as soon as it reaches that critical stage.

Be flexible about pasta types. Often, you can substitute one kind of pasta for another if you feel like a change, or if you don't happen to have the type called for in the recipe. When macaroni is called for, it's perfectly all right to use other small pasta shapes (such as sea shells). And if you like the color of spinach noodles or the chewiness of whole wheat noodles, you can use them in recipes calling for fettuccine—taking into account, of course, how these pastas would look and taste with the ingredients in the sauce.

Use pasta for quick side dishes. Pasta is a quick and versatile accompaniment for broiled meats or other entrées. Hot buttered macaroni, wide egg noodles with a sprinkling of poppy seeds, fettuccine or spaghetti with a simple olive oil and garlic coating—these and many others make easy and delicious side dishes.

Cook rice properly. If the rice you buy is marked "enriched," don't rinse it before cooking or drain it afterwards—this will wash away all the nutrients that have been added to the grain. Just cook according to package directions.

Tagliarini with Garlic Sauce

Simmering mellows the garlicky tomato sauce

To complete the meal, we suggest buttered green beans and a light red wine.

- 1 **package (8 oz.) tagliarini or fettuccine**
  Boiling salted water
- 1 **can (15 oz.) Italian-style tomatoes**
- 1 **teaspoon dry basil**
- ¾ **teaspoon salt**
- ¼ **teaspoon** *each* **crushed red pepper and freshly ground black pepper**
- ⅓ **cup olive oil**
- 6 **large cloves garlic, minced or pressed**
  Grated Parmesan cheese

Following package directions, cook tagliarini in a large kettle of boiling salted water until *al dente*; drain thoroughly.

Meanwhile, in a bowl, combine tomatoes (break up with a spoon) and their liquid, basil, salt, red pepper, and black pepper; set aside.

Place oil and garlic in a 1-quart pan. Cook over medium-low heat, stirring occasionally, until oil bubbles gently and garlic is light gold (do not brown garlic or it will taste bitter). Add tomato mixture to pan and simmer, uncovered, stirring occasionally, for 5 minutes.

Place hot tagliarini in a serving bowl, pour sauce over top, and toss gently. Pass cheese at the table to sprinkle over individual portions. Makes 4 servings.

Fettuccine with Walnut Sauce

Toasted nuts flavor the creamy sauce

To complete the meal, we suggest a spinach salad and buttered baby carrots.

- 1½ **cups coarsely chopped walnuts**
- 1 **package (8 oz.) fettuccine**
  Boiling salted water
- ½ **pint (1 cup) whipping cream**
- 1 **small clove garlic, minced or pressed**
- ¼ **teaspoon** *each* **salt and white pepper**
  About 2 tablespoons butter or margarine
  Grated Parmesan cheese

Spread walnuts in a shallow pan and bake in a 350° oven for 10 to 12 minutes or until lightly browned; cool slightly.

Following package directions, cook fettuccine in a large kettle of boiling salted water until *al dente*; drain thoroughly. Meanwhile, in a blender or food processor, combine walnuts, cream, garlic, salt, and pepper; whirl, using on-off bursts, until walnuts are coarsely ground.

Place hot drained pasta in a serving bowl and toss with butter until well coated. Top with walnut sauce; toss gently. Serve immediately. Pass cheese at the table to sprinkle on individual portions. Makes 4 servings.

Garden Vegetable Fettuccine

Whole wheat pasta with a crunchy vegetable sauce

To complete the meal, we suggest broiled Italian sausages and a carafe of wine.

- 8 **ounces whole wheat fettuccine**
  Boiling salted water
- 6 **strips bacon, cut into ½-inch pieces**
- 3 **cloves garlic, minced or pressed**
- 1 **large onion, chopped**
- 1 **large zucchini, cut into ½-inch cubes**
- 1 **small red or green bell pepper, seeded and chopped**
- 3 **large tomatoes, cut into ½-inch cubes**
- ½ **cup chopped parsley**
- ½ **cup chopped fresh basil leaves or 2 tablespoons dry basil**
- 2 **tablespoons olive oil or salad oil**
  Salt and pepper
  Grated Parmesan cheese

Following package directions, cook fettuccine in a large kettle of boiling salted water until *al dente*; drain thoroughly.

Meanwhile, in a wide frying pan over medium heat, cook bacon until crisp. Remove bacon from pan, drain, and set aside. Discard all but 2 tablespoons drippings. Add garlic and onion to pan and cook, stirring, until soft. Add zucchini and bell pepper; increase heat to medium-high and stir-fry until zucchini is tender-crisp (about 2 minutes). Add tomatoes, parsley, basil, and oil. Cook, stirring, until heated through; season to taste with salt and pepper.

Place hot fettuccine in a serving bowl; spoon sauce over top, sprinkle with bacon, and toss gently. Pass cheese at the table to sprinkle over individual portions. Makes 4 servings.

Macaroni & Cheese

An extra-cheesy version of the old standby

To complete the meal, we suggest a green salad and crunchy stir-fried vegetables.

>   1 package (1 lb.) small elbow macaroni
>   Boiling salted water
>   ½ cup (¼ lb.) butter or margarine
>   1 cup milk
>   4 cups (1 lb.) shredded sharp Cheddar cheese
>   ¼ teaspoon paprika
>   Salt and pepper

Following package directions, cook macaroni in a large kettle of boiling salted water until *al dente*; drain thoroughly. Melt butter in kettle over medium-high heat; add milk, drained macaroni, cheese, and paprika. Cook, stirring, until cheese is melted. Season to taste with salt and pepper. Makes 4 to 6 servings.

Curried Pasta Pilaf

Pilaf of tiny pasta looks almost like rice

To complete the meal, we suggest sliced cucumber salad, steamed broccoli, and buttered rolls.

>   4 tablespoons butter or margarine
>   1 large onion, chopped
>   1 large clove garlic, minced or pressed
>   2 medium-size tomatoes, seeded and chopped
>   1½ to 2 teaspoons curry powder
>   ½ teaspoon *each* salt and ground cumin
>   ¼ cup water
>   8 ounces (about 1⅓ cups) tiny pasta (anellini, pastina, puntalette, or stellini)
>   Boiling salted water
>   ¾ cup frozen peas
>   ½ pound small cooked shrimp

In a wide frying pan over medium heat, melt butter. Add onion and garlic and cook, stirring occasionally, until onion is soft. Add tomatoes, curry powder, salt, cumin, and water; cover and simmer for 10 minutes.

Meanwhile, following package directions, cook pasta in a large kettle of boiling salted water until *al dente*; drain thoroughly.

Add peas to tomato mixture. Bring to a boil over high heat; stir in pasta. Remove from heat and stir in shrimp. Makes 4 servings.

Indonesian Bamie

A spicy stir-fried pasta treat

Pictured on facing page

To complete the meal, we suggest iced tea or beer, and sliced pineapple or melon wedges.

Hint for the cook: Deveining shrimp is best done under cool running water; the water helps force out the sand vein.

>   1 package (8 oz.) vermicelli, broken in half
>   Boiling salted water
>   5 tablespoons salad oil
>   2 cloves garlic, minced or pressed
>   ½ teaspoon crushed red pepper
>   1 flank steak (about 1 lb.), cut across the grain into ⅛-inch-thick slices
>   ¼ pound medium-size raw shrimp, shelled, deveined, and cut in half lengthwise
>   2 green onions (including tops), cut diagonally into ½-inch slices
>   2 cups coarsely shredded green cabbage
>   1 cup *each* sliced (about ¼ inch thick) leeks and celery
>   ¼ cup soy sauce

Following package directions, cook vermicelli in a large kettle of boiling salted water until *al dente*; drain, rinse with cold water, and drain again. Set aside.

Place a wok or wide frying pan over high heat. When pan is hot, add 2 tablespoons of the oil. When oil begins to heat, add garlic and pepper and stir once. Add steak and stir-fry for 1 minute. Add shrimp and stir-fry until shrimp are opaque and steak is browned but still pink inside (about 30 seconds). Remove from pan.

Pour 2 more tablespoons oil into pan; add onions, cabbage, leeks, and celery. Stir-fry vegetables until tender-crisp (about 1½ minutes). Add vermicelli, remaining 1 tablespoon oil, and soy; stir-fry for 1 minute. Return meat mixture to pan and continue stir-frying until almost all liquid has evaporated. Makes 4 to 6 servings.

Pasta is popular everywhere, from Italy to Asia. This version from the islands of Indonesia is chock-full of shrimp, beef, and crunchy vegetables. It's called Bamie (recipe on this page).

Tuna Carbonara

Parmesan and red bell pepper flavor this pasta

To complete the meal, we suggest a quick vegetable (see pages 52–53) and a crisp green salad.

>   1 package (8 oz.) vermicelli
>   Boiling salted water
>   2 tablespoons butter or margarine
>   2 tablespoons olive oil
>   1 large red bell pepper, seeded and cut into thin strips, or 1 can (7 oz.) whole pimentos, drained and cut into thin strips
>   3 cloves garlic, minced or pressed
>   1 can (9¼ oz.) chunk-style tuna, drained and flaked
>   4 eggs
>   1 cup (3 oz.) grated Parmesan cheese
>   ¼ cup chopped parsley
>   Salt and pepper

Following package directions, cook vermicelli in a large kettle of boiling salted water until *al dente.* Drain, rinse with cold water, and drain again.

Meanwhile, in a wide frying pan over medium-high heat, melt butter in oil. Add bell pepper and garlic; cook, stirring, until pepper is soft. Add vermicelli and tuna; cook, stirring constantly, until heated through. Remove from heat. In a bowl, lightly beat eggs; pour over vermicelli mixture, then add cheese and parsley. Toss gently with two forks until pasta is evenly coated; season to taste with salt and pepper. Serve immediately. Makes 4 servings.

Linguine with Clam Sauce

Clams abound in a creamy Parmesan-butter sauce

To complete the meal, we suggest Lemon-Dill Green Beans (page 52); serve fruit for dessert.

>   1 package (8 oz.) linguine
>   Boiling salted water
>   4 tablespoons butter or margarine
>   2 tablespoons olive oil or salad oil
>   3 cloves garlic, minced or pressed
>   ½ cup half-and-half (light cream)
>   3 cans (6½ oz. *each*) chopped clams, drained
>   ¼ cup finely chopped parsley
>   ½ cup grated Parmesan cheese
>   Salt and pepper

Following package directions, cook linguine in a large kettle of boiling salted water until *al dente;* drain thoroughly.

Meanwhile, in a wide frying pan over medium heat, melt butter in oil. Add garlic and cook, stirring, for 2 minutes. Stir in half-and-half and clams and heat through, but do not boil.

Place hot linguine in a serving bowl; pour clam mixture over top. Add parsley and cheese and toss until well combined. Serve immediately. Makes 4 servings.

Macaroni with Meat & Yogurt

Beef on a bed of pasta with creamy yogurt sauce

To complete the meal, we suggest sliced tomatoes and cucumbers in a vinaigrette dressing.

>   1½ cups large elbow or small shell macaroni
>   Boiling salted water
>   2 tablespoons pine nuts or slivered almonds
>   1 tablespoon butter or margarine
>   1 small onion, chopped
>   ½ pound lean ground beef
>   1 teaspoon salt
>   ¼ teaspoon ground cinnamon
>   ⅛ teaspoon *each* pepper and ground nutmeg
>   1 egg
>   ½ pint (1 cup) plain yogurt
>   1 clove garlic, minced or pressed

Following package directions, cook macaroni in a large kettle of boiling salted water until *al dente;* drain thoroughly.

Meanwhile, in a wide frying pan over medium heat, cook pine nuts, stirring, until golden (about 5 minutes); remove from pan and set aside. Add butter to pan; when melted, add onion and cook, stirring, until soft. Crumble beef into pan and cook, stirring, until browned. Stir in ½ teaspoon of the salt, cinnamon, pepper, nutmeg, and pine nuts. Cover and keep warm.

In a 2-quart pan, lightly beat egg; beat in yogurt, garlic, and remaining ½ teaspoon salt. Stir constantly over medium heat until heated through but not simmering; remove from heat. Add hot drained macaroni and stir until well combined. Pour into a shallow serving dish and top with meat mixture. Makes 3 or 4 servings.

Spaghetti with Chicken Livers

An Italian classic, simplified

To complete the meal, we suggest bread sticks, sautéed zucchini, and red wine.

    1 package (8 oz.) spaghetti
       Boiling salted water
    ½ cup (¼ lb.) butter or margarine
    ½ pound mushrooms, sliced
    4 green onions (including tops), sliced
    ¼ cup chopped parsley
    ¼ cup Marsala or white wine
    1 pound chicken livers, cut in half

Following package directions, cook spaghetti in a large kettle of boiling salted water until *al dente*; drain thoroughly.

Meanwhile, in a wide frying pan over medium-high heat, melt butter. Add mushrooms and onions and cook, stirring, until vegetables are soft (2 to 3 minutes). Add parsley, Marsala, and livers. Cook, stirring often, until livers are just firm but still slightly pink in center when slashed (about 5 minutes).

Place hot drained spaghetti in a serving bowl and toss with chicken liver mixture until well combined. Makes 4 servings.

Salami & Mushroom Spaghetti

Pizza toppers can also enhance spaghetti

To complete the meal, we suggest a romaine salad and bread sticks or crusty rolls.

    1 package (8 oz.) spaghetti
       Boiling salted water
    3 tablespoons butter or margarine
    1 package (about 4 oz.) sliced Italian dry salami, cut into thin strips
    ½ pound mushrooms, thinly sliced
    4 green onions (including tops), thinly sliced
    ½ cup half-and-half (light cream)
    ½ cup grated Parmesan cheese

Following package directions, cook spaghetti in a large kettle of boiling salted water until *al dente*; drain thoroughly.

Meanwhile, in a wide frying pan over medium-high heat, melt butter. Add salami, mushrooms, and onions; cook, stirring frequently, until mushrooms are soft and liquid has evaporated.

Reduce heat to low, add half-and-half, and cook until mixture is heated through. Add hot drained spaghetti and lightly toss with sauce; then add cheese. Toss until spaghetti is evenly coated. Makes 4 servings.

Green Noodles Supreme

Spinach noodles in a creamy sauce with ham

To complete the meal, we suggest crusty rolls and a chilled white wine.

Hint for the cook: If you can't find green noodles in your market, substitute regular fettuccine.

    1 package (8 oz.) medium-wide green noodles
       Boiling salted water
    4 tablespoons butter or margarine
    ¼ pound mushrooms, sliced
    1 clove garlic, minced or pressed
    6 ounces cooked ham, cut into julienne strips (about 1 cup)
    ¾ cup whipping cream
    1 cup frozen peas
    ¼ teaspoon ground nutmeg
       Salt and pepper
       Grated Parmesan cheese

Following package directions, cook noodles in a large kettle of boiling salted water until *al dente*; drain thoroughly.

Meanwhile, in a wide frying pan over medium heat, melt butter. Add mushrooms, garlic, and ham; cook, stirring often, until mushrooms are soft and lightly browned. Stir in cream and peas; bring to a boil and cook, stirring constantly, until sauce thickens slightly and forms large, shiny bubbles (2 to 3 minutes). Stir in nutmeg. Pour hot drained noodles into pan; toss lightly until evenly coated. Season to taste with salt and pepper. Serve immediately; pass cheese at the table to sprinkle over individual portions. Makes 4 servings.

Pasta Twists with Sausage & Cream

Bits of sausage cling to corkscrew-shaped pasta

To complete the meal, we suggest a colorful antipasto platter.

> 1 package (8 oz.) rotelle or other pasta twists
> Boiling salted water
> 4 tablespoons butter or margarine
> ½ pound mild Italian sausage
> ¾ cup whipping cream
> ¼ cup *each* dry white wine and grated Parmesan cheese
> Ground nutmeg
> Grated Parmesan cheese

Following package directions, cook pasta in a large kettle of boiling salted water until *al dente*; drain thoroughly.

Meanwhile, in a wide frying pan over medium-low heat, melt butter. Remove casings from sausage and crumble meat into pan; cook, stirring occasionally, until meat is lightly browned. Increase heat to medium-high. Add cream and wine and bring to a boil. Boil gently, stirring constantly, until sauce thickens slightly and forms large, shiny bubbles (2 to 3 minutes). Add hot drained pasta; then remove from heat and add the ¼ cup cheese. Toss until pasta is evenly coated. Sprinkle lightly with nutmeg and serve immediately. Pass additional cheese at the table to sprinkle over individual portions. Makes 3 or 4 servings.

Rigatoni with Zucchini & Kielbasa

Chunky pasta, juicy sausage, and tender zucchini

To complete the meal, we suggest crusty bread, beer, and Fresh Raspberry Sundaes (page 92).

> 2 cups rigatoni or large elbow macaroni
> Boiling salted water
> Dijon Herb Sauce (recipe follows)
> 2 kielbasa (Polish sausages) or other fully cooked sausages (about 12 oz. *total*), cut into ¼-inch slices
> 1 medium-size red onion, thinly sliced
> 3 small zucchini, thinly sliced

In a wide frying pan, cook rigatoni in 1 inch of boiling salted water until *al dente* (10 to 15 minutes); drain thoroughly and set aside. Meanwhile, prepare Dijon Herb Sauce; set aside.

Rinse and dry pan and place over medium-high heat. Add sausages and cook, stirring, for 1 minute. Add onion and cook, stirring, until soft (about 3 more minutes). Stir in zucchini and cook, stirring, just until tender-crisp (about 2 more minutes). Add cooked pasta and Dijon Herb Sauce and continue cooking and stirring until mixture is heated through (1 to 2 more minutes). Makes 4 servings.

Dijon Herb Sauce. In a small bowl, combine ¼ cup **red wine vinegar** and 2 tablespoons *each* **Dijon mustard** and **dry basil.**

Skillet Spanish Rice

Chorizo sausage gives this dish its zing

To complete the meal, we suggest a crisp lettuce and avocado salad, and hot buttered tortillas.

> About ¾ pound chorizo sausage
> 1 large onion, chopped
> 1 large green pepper, seeded and cut into 1-inch squares
> 1 cup long-grain white rice
> 1½ cups tomato juice
> 2 cups water
> 1 teaspoon sugar
> 1 can (2¼ oz.) sliced ripe olives, drained
> 2 cups (8 oz.) shredded sharp Cheddar cheese

Remove casings from sausage and crumble meat into a wide frying pan with an ovenproof handle. Cook over medium-high heat, stirring, until browned (about 5 minutes); spoon off and discard fat. Add onion and green pepper and cook until onion is soft (about 5 more minutes).

Stir in rice, tomato juice, water, and sugar; bring to a boil and boil for 5 minutes, stirring often. Reserve a few olive slices for garnish; stir remaining olives into rice mixture. Cover, reduce heat, and cook until rice is *al dente* (about 20 minutes).

Remove from heat, sprinkle cheese evenly over top, and broil 6 inches below heat just until cheese is melted and beginning to brown (about 3 minutes). Garnish with reserved olive slices. Makes 4 to 6 servings.

Chile & Cheese Rice

Creamy rice gets a little zip from green chiles

To complete the meal, we suggest broccoli, red cabbage salad, and iced tea.

- 2 cups water
- ½ teaspoon salt
- 1 cup long-grain white rice
- 1 can (4 oz.) whole green chiles, drained, seeded, and diced
- 1 jar (2 oz.) diced pimentos, drained
- ½ pint (1 cup) sour cream
- 1 cup *each* shredded jack cheese and Cheddar cheese (8 oz. *total*)

Place water and salt in a 2-quart pan; bring to a boil over high heat. Add rice and cover. When water resumes a full rolling boil, reduce heat and simmer until rice is *al dente* and all liquid is absorbed (about 20 minutes). Stir in chiles, pimentos, sour cream, jack cheese, and ½ cup of the Cheddar cheese. Pour rice mixture into a greased shallow 1½-quart casserole; sprinkle remaining ½ cup Cheddar cheese over top. Bake, uncovered, in a 350° oven for 30 minutes. Makes 4 servings.

Fried Rice with Ham & Peanuts

From China, a quick meal using leftover meat

To complete the meal, we suggest cooked Chinese pea pods, hot tea, and fortune cookies.

- 2 cups cold cooked long-grain white rice
- 2 eggs
- ¼ teaspoon salt
- 4 tablespoons salad oil
- 1 small onion, chopped
- 1 clove garlic, minced or pressed
- 1 medium-size green pepper, seeded and diced
- ¼ pound mushrooms, diced
- ½ pound cold cooked ham, chicken, turkey, or pork, diced (about 1½ cups)
- ½ cup salted peanuts
- 2 tablespoons soy sauce

Rub cooked rice with wet hands so all grains are separated; set aside. In a small bowl, lightly beat together eggs and salt. Heat 1 tablespoon of the oil in a wok or wide frying pan over medium heat. Add eggs and cook, stirring occasionally, until soft curds form; remove from pan and set aside.

Increase heat to medium-high; add 1 more tablespoon oil to pan. Add onion and garlic and cook, stirring, until onion is soft; then add green pepper, mushrooms, ham, and peanuts. Stir-fry until heated through (about 2 minutes). Remove from pan and set aside.

Heat remaining 2 tablespoons oil in pan. Add rice and stir-fry until heated through (about 2 minutes); stir in ham mixture and soy. Add eggs; stir mixture gently until eggs are in small pieces. Makes 4 servings.

Lamb & Spinach Pilaf

A flavorful meat mixture tops cracked wheat

To complete the meal, we suggest sliced tomatoes in a yogurt dressing, and dried fruit for dessert.

- 2¼ cups regular-strength beef broth
- 1 cup cracked wheat (bulgur)
- 1 bunch (about ¾ lb.) spinach
- ½ teaspoon salt
- 1 pound lean ground lamb
- 1 large onion, chopped
- ½ teaspoon ground cinnamon
- ⅓ cup water
- ½ cup raisins
- Pepper

In a small pan, bring broth to a boil over high heat. Add cracked wheat, then cover pan. When broth resumes a full rolling boil, reduce heat and simmer until grains are *al dente* and liquid is absorbed (15 to 20 minutes). Meanwhile, remove and discard tough spinach stems; wash leaves, pat dry, and cut into 1-inch-wide strips. Set aside.

Sprinkle salt into a wide frying pan over medium heat. Crumble lamb into pan; cook, stirring, until meat begins to brown. Add onion, cinnamon, water, and raisins; cover and simmer for 5 minutes. Stir spinach into meat mixture; cover and cook just until spinach is wilted (1 to 2 minutes). Remove from heat and season to taste with pepper.

Mound hot cracked wheat on a platter and top with meat mixture. Makes 4 to 6 servings.

Quick Vegetable Ideas

Complement a speedy entrée with a quickly cooked vegetable, seasoned just right. Here's a collection of dishes to add color, texture, and fresh flavor to your menus.

These recipes are versatile—you can enjoy the seasonings and toppings we suggest with a variety of vegetables. When asparagus is in season, try Asparagus with Cashew Butter; later in the year, spoon the savory hot butter over cooked green beans. And the crumb topping for Broccoli Polonaise can also enhance cauliflower and spinach.

Asparagus with Cashew Butter

Snap off and discard tough ends from 2 pounds **asparagus;** rinse spears well. In a wide frying pan, bring 1 inch **water** to a boil over high heat. Layer asparagus spears evenly in pan; then cover, reduce heat, and cook until asparagus is just tender when pierced (7 to 10 minutes). Drain well.

Meanwhile, in a small pan over low heat, melt 4 tablespoons **butter** or margarine. Stir in 2 teaspoons **lemon juice,** ¼ teaspoon **marjoram leaves,** and ¼ cup **roasted, salted cashews,** coarsely chopped. Simmer for 2 to 3 minutes, then pour over hot cooked asparagus. Makes 4 servings.

Broccoli Polonaise

Trim and discard tough stalk bases from 1 to 1½ pounds **broccoli.** Peel stalks and cut lengthwise into uniform spears; then rinse.

In a wide frying pan, bring 1 inch **water** to a boil over high heat. Add broccoli; then cover, reduce heat, and cook until broccoli stalks are just tender when pierced (7 to 12 minutes). Drain well.

Meanwhile, in a small pan over medium heat, melt 5 tablespoons **butter** or margarine. Add ½ cup **fine dry bread crumbs** and stir until browned. Remove from heat; stir in 1 **hard-cooked egg,** chopped, and 1 tablespoon *each* thinly sliced **green onion** (including top) and minced **parsley.** Sprinkle crumb mixture over hot broccoli. Makes 4 to 6 servings.

Cream-glazed Anise Carrots
Pictured on page 87

In a wide frying pan over high heat, melt 2 tablespoons **butter** or margarine. Add 3 cups thinly sliced **carrots,** 3 tablespoons **water,** and ¼ teaspoon **anise seeds** (crushed). Cover and cook, stirring often and adding more water if necessary, until carrots are just tender-crisp (4 to 7 minutes). Add 3 tablespoons **whipping cream** and cook, uncovered, stirring constantly, until liquid has almost evaporated. Season to taste with **salt** and **pepper.** Makes 4 or 5 servings.

Lemon-Dill Green Beans

Remove ends from 1 pound **green beans.** Rinse beans, then cut crosswise into 1-inch pieces. In a wide frying pan over high heat, melt 2 tablespoons **butter** or margarine; add beans and 5 to 6 tablespoons **water.** Cover and cook, stirring often, until beans are tender-crisp (4 to 7 minutes). Stir in 1 tablespoon minced **parsley,** 1 more tablespoon **butter** or margarine, 2 teaspoons **lemon juice,** and ¼ to ½ teaspoon **dill weed.** Season to taste with **salt** and **pepper;** heat through. Makes 4 or 5 servings.

Mushrooms au Gratin

Wash 1 pound **mushrooms,** then cut them lengthwise through stems into ¼-inch-thick slices. In a wide frying pan over medium-high heat, melt 2 tablespoons **butter** or margarine. Add mushrooms and cook, stirring often, until mushrooms are lightly browned but not all liquid has evaporated (3 to 5 minutes).

Meanwhile, in a small bowl, combine ⅓ cup **sour cream,** 2 teaspoons **all-purpose flour,** and a dash *each* of **salt** and **pepper.** Stir until smooth, then stir into mushrooms. Cook, stirring, until mixture boils. Remove from heat and sprinkle ¼ cup minced **parsley** and ½ cup shredded **Swiss or Cheddar cheese** evenly over top. Cover pan and let stand until cheese is melted (3 to 4 minutes). Makes about 4 servings.

Peas in Pods

Pictured on page 79

Rinse 2 pounds whole **unshelled peas;** do not dry. Place in a 5-quart kettle and add 2 tablespoons **water;** then cover kettle and place over medium-high heat. Cook, stirring well every 5 minutes, until peas are tender to bite (about 15 minutes—shell a few to test). Pour into a warm serving bowl.

To eat, hold a whole pod at one end and put it in your mouth. Bite lightly at the end you're holding, then pull pod through your teeth—peas pop into your mouth. (Or, let diners shell their own peas at the table.) Makes 4 servings.

Baked Potato Sticks

Pictured on page 79

Scrub 1 large **russet potato;** cut lengthwise into eighths. Brush with melted **butter** or margarine; sprinkle with **garlic salt** and **oregano leaves.** Arrange spears, skin side down, 1 inch apart on a baking sheet. Bake in a 425° oven for 30 minutes or until tender. Makes 2 servings.

Baked Sweet Potato Sticks

Prepare **Baked Potato Sticks,** substituting 1 large **sweet potato** or yam for russet potato; use **ground nutmeg** in place of garlic salt and oregano leaves. Decrease baking time to 25 minutes.

Shredded Rutabagas

In a wide frying pan over medium-high heat, melt 3 tablespoons **butter** or margarine. Add 2 cups coarsely shredded, firmly packed **rutabagas,** 2 tablespoons **water,** 1 to 1½ tablespoons firmly packed **brown sugar,** and 1 teaspoon **soy sauce.** Cover and cook, stirring often, until tender-crisp (about 5 minutes). Makes 3 or 4 servings.

Skillet Squash

Trim ends from 6 medium-size **zucchini** or other summer squash; rinse and cut crosswise into ¼-inch slices. Set aside. Heat 3 tablespoons **olive oil,** butter, or margarine in a wide frying pan over medium-high heat; add 1 clove **garlic** (minced or pressed) and cook, stirring, for 2 to 3 minutes. Add squash and cook, uncovered, stirring often, until squash is just tender-crisp (3 to 5 minutes). Stir in 1 tablespoon *each* minced **parsley** and sliced **green onion** (including top), 1 teaspoon **oregano leaves,** and ¼ teaspoon **sugar.** Season to taste with **salt** and **pepper.** Cook, stirring, until squash and seasonings are well blended (1 to 2 more minutes). Makes 4 to 6 servings.

Broiled Tomatoes Parmesan

Cut 6 medium-size **tomatoes** in half crosswise, then sprinkle cut surfaces with **pepper** and **dry basil.** Top each half with ½ teaspoon grated **Parmesan cheese** and dot with ½ teaspoon soft **butter** or margarine.

Place on a rack in a broiler pan; broil about 6 inches below heat for 3 to 4 minutes or until lightly browned. Makes 6 servings.

Glazed Turnips

In a wide frying pan, combine 2 cups thinly sliced **turnips,** 2 tablespoons **butter** or margarine, 2 tablespoons **water,** and 1 tablespoon **sugar.** Cover and cook over medium-high heat, stirring often, until turnips are just tender when pierced (about 5 minutes). Uncover and cook until glazed. Makes 4 servings.

Seafood

For greater efficiency:

Purchase fresh fish carefully. Always buy the freshest fish you can find. The flesh of whole fish should spring back when gently pressed, and the eyes should be clear and full, not sunken. When shopping for fillets and steaks, look for moist, firm flesh. Of course, avoid any fish that has a strong, fishy smell—truly fresh fish has a mild and delicate aroma.

Buy the right amount. Uncooked fish doesn't keep well, so to avoid waste, buy just as much as you need and cook it within 2 days. Allow ⅓ to ½ pound boneless fish per serving.

Store fish properly. To keep fish fresh, wrap it in a leakproof wrapper and refrigerate at 35° to 40° as soon as possible after purchase—even a couple of hours at room temperature can allow spoilage to begin.

Use your leftovers. If you have leftover fish, use it to make salad or sandwich fillings for lunch or supper the next day. Cooked fish may be kept in the refrigerator, covered, for up to 3 days—no longer.

Keep frozen fish on hand. Packaged frozen fish—sole, perch, cod, and haddock—is available in many markets; it's usually sold in 1-pound blocks. Frozen fish is useful if you live in an area where fresh fish isn't readily available, or if you don't have time to shop and need a spur-of-the-moment dinner. Since frozen fish can be cooked without defrosting (see Foil-wrapped Fish with Butter Sauce, page 56, or Fish-in-a-Hurry, facing page), it can be really helpful when time is short.

You can also substitute thawed frozen fish for fresh. The night before you plan to cook it, move fish from freezer to refrigerator; it will be thawed and ready to use by the next evening. Before cooking thawed fish, be sure to pat it dry with paper towels.

Get more juice from lemons. Lemons, so often used in fish cookery, yield more juice if you know how to handle them. For highest yield, use room-temperature lemons rather than refrigerated ones. Before cutting the fruit open to squeeze out the juice, roll it between your palms, pressing gently.

Fish-in-a-Hurry

From freezer to table in 20 minutes

To complete the meal, we suggest a sliced cucumber salad and dinner rolls.

     Tomato-Caper Sauce (page 60)
1 **package (1 lb., about 1 inch thick) frozen fish fillets (sole, perch, cod, or haddock), unthawed**
     Olive oil or salad oil
     Salt and pepper
     Yellow cornmeal

Prepare Tomato-Caper Sauce and keep warm.

    Generously rub frozen fish block with oil; sprinkle all sides with salt and pepper, then coat heavily with cornmeal. Place on a greased baking pan and broil 4 inches below heat for 6 minutes; turn fish block over and broil until crust is deep golden brown and flesh inside is just opaque when fish is prodded with a fork (2 to 4 more minutes).

    Transfer fish to a platter. Pour sauce into a serving bowl and pass at the table to spoon over individual servings. Makes 2 or 3 servings.

Creamy Dilled Fish Fillets

Fish baked in a dilly sour cream sauce

To complete the meal, we suggest hot pumpernickel bread and a spinach-and-tomato salad.

1 **pound fish fillets or steaks (halibut, ling cod, red snapper, perch, or sea bass), _each_ about 1 inch thick**
     Salt and pepper
¾ **cup sour cream**
⅓ **cup mayonnaise**
2 **tablespoons _each_ all-purpose flour and lemon juice**
¼ **teaspoon dill weed**
     Paprika
     Fresh dill or parsley sprigs

Cut fish into serving-size pieces and arrange in a single layer in a 9 by 13-inch baking dish; sprinkle lightly with salt and pepper.

    In a small bowl, combine sour cream, mayonnaise, flour, lemon juice, and dill; stir until smooth and well blended. Spread sour cream mixture over fish. Bake, uncovered, in a 400° oven for 10 to 12 minutes or until flesh inside is just opaque when fish is prodded in thickest portion

with a fork. Sprinkle with paprika and garnish with dill sprigs. Makes 2 or 3 servings.

Sautéed Sesame Fish

Sesame-coated fillets with a tangy lemon relish

To complete the meal, we suggest poppy seed rolls and steamed broccoli.

     Lemon Relish (recipe follows)
2 **pounds firm-textured white fish fillets (halibut, rockfish, swordfish, or turbot), _each_ about 1 inch thick**
     Salt and pepper
¼ **cup all-purpose flour**
½ **cup fine dry bread crumbs**
¼ **cup sesame seeds**
1 **egg**
2 **tablespoons milk**
     About 4 tablespoons butter or margarine
     About 4 tablespoons salad oil

Prepare Lemon Relish and set aside. Cut fish into serving-size pieces; sprinkle with salt and pepper and dust lightly with flour. In a rimmed plate or pie pan, combine bread crumbs and sesame seeds; in another rimmed plate or pie pan, beat egg with milk until well combined.

    Dip fish pieces in egg mixture to cover. Drain briefly; then coat completely with crumb mixture, shaking off excess.

    In a wide frying pan over medium heat, melt 2 tablespoons of the butter in 2 tablespoons of the oil. When butter mixture sizzles, add as many pieces of fish as will fit without crowding; cook, turning once, until flesh inside is just opaque when fish is prodded in thickest portion with a fork (8 to 10 minutes _total_). Transfer fish to a platter, cover, and keep warm; cook remaining fish, adding more butter and oil as needed.

    At the table, pass Lemon Relish to spoon over individual servings. Makes 4 to 6 servings.

Lemon Relish. In a small bowl, combine ½ cup finely chopped **green onions** (including tops) and ¼ cup _each_ **lemon juice** and **chopped parsley**.

Baked Fish in Vegetable Sauce

Colorful, tomatoey sauce keeps fish moist

To complete the meal, we suggest Brussels sprouts and hot buttered noodles.

> 2½ pounds fish fillets or steaks (halibut, ling cod, rockfish, swordfish, or turbot), *each* about 1 inch thick
> 4 tablespoons butter, margarine, or olive oil
> 1 large onion, finely chopped
> 2 cloves garlic, minced or pressed
> 1 cup *each* finely chopped carrots and celery
> ¼ cup minced parsley
> 1½ teaspoons *each* dry basil and oregano leaves
> 1 bay leaf
> ½ cup regular-strength chicken broth
> ½ cup dry white wine or regular-strength chicken broth
> 1 can (about 28 oz.) Italian-style tomatoes
> Salt and pepper
> Lemon juice
> Parsley sprigs

Cut fish into serving-size pieces; place in a greased 10 by 15-inch baking pan and set aside.

In a wide frying pan over medium heat, melt butter. Add onion and garlic and cook, stirring occasionally, until onion is soft. Stir in carrots, celery, parsley, basil, oregano, bay leaf, and broth. Bring to a boil; then cover, reduce heat, and simmer until vegetables are tender (about 10 minutes).

Add wine and tomatoes (break up with a spoon) and their liquid. Increase heat to medium-high and cook, stirring, until sauce is thick. Season to taste with salt, pepper, and lemon juice. Spoon sauce over and around fish in pan. Bake, uncovered, in a 375° oven for 20 to 25 minutes or until flesh inside is just opaque when fish is prodded in thickest portion with a fork.

Transfer fish to a platter; spoon sauce over and around fish. Garnish with parsley sprigs. Makes 6 servings.

Foil-wrapped Fish with Butter Sauce

Fish in foil packets steams in its own juices

To complete the meal, we suggest sautéed mushrooms, hot rolls, and red and green pepper strips in vinaigrette.

> 2 pounds fish fillets or steaks (halibut, ling cod, or rockfish), or two 1-pound (about 1 inch thick) packages frozen fish (sole, perch, cod, or haddock), unthawed
> 2 tablespoons chopped onion
> 1 tablespoon chopped parsley
> Almond Browned Butter (optional; page 60)

Place fresh fish pieces, slightly overlapping, on a piece of foil large enough to enclose them. (If using frozen fish, leave blocks whole.) Sprinkle fish evenly with onion and parsley; wrap in foil, crimping edges to keep in all juices.

Place on a baking sheet in a 425° oven, or on a rack in a covered steamer over about 1 inch of boiling water. Cook until flesh inside is just opaque when fish is prodded in thickest portion with a fork (allow 12 to 15 minutes for fillets or steaks, 25 to 30 minutes for blocks of frozen fish). Meanwhile, prepare Almond Browned Butter (if used).

When fish is done, open foil. Transfer fish to a platter and keep warm; drain off liquid accumulated in foil and discard. Pass butter sauce at the table to spoon over individual servings. Makes 4 to 6 servings.

Wine-poached Halibut

A light, buttery sauce crowns moist halibut steaks

To complete the meal, we suggest Broiled Tomatoes Parmesan (page 53) and rice.

> 3 large halibut steaks, *each* about 1 pound and 1¼ inches thick
> ½ cup dry white wine or regular-strength chicken broth
> 3 tablespoons lemon juice
> 4 tablespoons butter or margarine
> ½ cup thinly sliced green onions (including tops)
> Salt and pepper

Cut halibut steaks in half lengthwise along center bone; discard bone. Arrange the 6 portions side by side in a greased 9 by 13-inch baking pan; pour in wine and lemon juice. Cover tightly with foil and bake in a 375° oven for 15 to 20 minutes or until flesh inside is just opaque when fish is prodded in thickest portion with a fork.

Lift fish from pan with a slotted spatula and arrange on a platter; keep warm. Add butter and onions to juices in pan; then place pan over medium-high heat and bring butter mixture to a boil. Boil, stirring occasionally, until reduced to ½ cup. Season to taste with salt and pepper and spoon over fish. Makes 6 servings.

Fish & Mushroom Skewers

Decorative spears of fish and whole mushrooms

To complete the meal, we suggest Lemon-Dill Green Beans (page 52) and rice.

> **Tartar Sauce (optional; page 60)**
> 16 whole bay leaves
> 1¼ pounds swordfish or halibut steaks, *each* about 1¼ inch thick
> 16 large mushrooms
> 4 tablespoons butter or margarine
> ½ teaspoon *each* paprika and dry chervil

Prepare Tartar Sauce (if used) and set aside.

Place bay leaves in a small bowl, add enough hot water to cover, and let stand for 5 minutes to soften; drain. Cut fish steaks into 1¼-inch squares. Thread fish squares, bay leaves, and mushrooms alternately on 4 metal or long bamboo skewers.

In a small pan over medium heat, melt butter with paprika and chervil. Evenly brush butter mixture over fish and mushrooms. Place skewers on a rack in a broiler pan and broil 4 inches below heat for 4 minutes; turn and broil until flesh inside is just opaque when fish is prodded with a fork (3 to 4 more minutes).

Transfer skewers to a platter; pass Tartar Sauce at the table. Makes 4 servings.

Swordfish Steaks with Mushrooms

Marinated fish with a lemony mushroom topping

To complete the meal, we suggest crunchy stir-fried vegetables and hot onion rolls.

> 3 tablespoons lemon juice
> ¼ cup dry white wine or water
> 1 clove garlic, minced or pressed
> ½ teaspoon *each* oregano leaves, salt, and pepper
> ¼ teaspoon fennel seeds, crushed
> 2 pounds swordfish steaks, *each* about ¾ inch thick
> 2 tablespoons olive oil or salad oil
> ½ pound mushrooms, sliced
> 2 or 3 green onions (including tops), thinly sliced

In a 9 by 13-inch dish, combine lemon juice, wine, garlic, oregano, salt, pepper, and fennel seeds. Add fish and let stand, turning occasionally, for 30 minutes. With a slotted spatula, lift fish from marinade, drain briefly (reserve marinade), and place in a greased broiler pan. Broil 4 inches below heat for 5 minutes; turn and broil until flesh inside is just opaque when fish is prodded in thickest portion with a fork (5 to 8 more minutes).

Meanwhile, heat oil in a frying pan over medium heat; add mushrooms and cook, stirring occasionally, until soft. Stir in reserved marinade and simmer for about 2 minutes. Transfer cooked fish to a platter; top with mushroom sauce and sprinkle with onions. Makes 4 to 6 servings.

Stuffed Sole Princess

Delicate sole fillets with a shrimp filling

To complete the meal, we suggest Garlic Toast (page 25), asparagus, and white wine.

> 4 large sole fillets (about 1½ lbs. *total*)
> ¼ pound small cooked shrimp
> Salt and pepper
> Paprika
> 1 tablespoon lemon juice
> ¼ cup dry white wine
> 2 tablespoons chopped green onion (including top)
> 1 clove garlic, minced or pressed
> 2 tablespoons butter or margarine
> 1 tablespoon all-purpose flour

Place fillets, skinned side down, on work surface. Place ¼ of the shrimp across one end of each fillet; roll each fillet into a cylinder and secure with a wooden pick. Place rolled fillets, seam side down, in a greased shallow baking dish. Sprinkle with salt, pepper, and paprika.

In a small bowl, stir together lemon juice, wine, onion, and garlic; pour over fish. Bake, covered, in a 350° oven for 25 minutes or until flesh inside is just opaque when fish is prodded in thickest portion with a fork. With a slotted spoon, transfer rolled fillets to a serving plate; reserve liquid from baking dish. Remove and discard picks from fish; cover fish and keep warm.

In a small pan over medium heat, melt butter. Stir in flour and cook, stirring, until bubbly. Remove pan from heat and gradually stir in liquid from baking dish. Return to heat and cook, stirring, until thickened. Pour sauce over rolled fillets. Makes 4 servings.

Salmon Steaks with Spinach

Elegant enough for company

Pictured on facing page

To complete the meal, we suggest buttered new potatoes, cucumber salad, and a chilled white wine.

  4 tablespoons butter or margarine
  1 large onion, chopped
  1 clove garlic, minced or pressed
  2 pounds spinach
    Salt and pepper
  4 salmon steaks, *each* about 1 inch thick
  1 teaspoon dill weed
    Lemon wedges

In a 5 to 6-quart kettle over medium heat, melt 3 tablespoons of the butter. Add onion and garlic and cook, stirring occasionally, until onion is very soft (about 15 minutes). Meanwhile, remove and discard tough spinach stems; wash leaves (do not pat dry) and cut into 1-inch-wide strips.

Stir spinach (with water that clings to leaves) into onion mixture. Cover kettle, increase heat to high, and cook until spinach is bright green and wilted (about 3 minutes). Uncover and cook until liquid has evaporated, stirring occasionally. Remove from heat; season to taste with salt and pepper. Transfer to a rimmed platter and keep warm.

Arrange salmon on a lightly greased baking pan; broil 4 inches below heat for 5 minutes. Turn steaks; sprinkle with salt, pepper, and dill and dot with remaining 1 tablespoon butter. Broil steaks for about 5 more minutes or until flesh inside is just opaque when fish is prodded in thickest portion with a fork. *(To grill salmon:* place steaks on a lightly greased range-top grill; cook for time specified in broiling instructions above, turning and seasoning with salt, pepper, dill, and butter after 5 minutes.)

To serve, place salmon steaks atop spinach and garnish with lemon wedges. Makes 4 servings.

Hot from a sizzling range-top grill, salmon steaks make an irresistible seafood entrée (they're also delicious cooked under the broiler). Arranged on an emerald bed of cooked spinach and garnished with lemon wedges, they'll tempt the most tenacious meat-and-potatoes lover. The recipe is on this page.

Bacon-stuffed Trout

Bacon flavor permeates this crusty baked fish

To complete the meal, we suggest Cream-glazed Anise Carrots (page 52), green salad, and bread or rolls.

  6 strips bacon
  1 large onion, chopped
  6 whole trout (about 8 oz. *each*), cleaned
  3 bay leaves, split lengthwise
  ¾ cup crushed seasoned croutons
  6 tablespoons grated Parmesan cheese
  ¼ teaspoon *each* garlic powder and pepper
  1 egg
  1 teaspoon water
  6 tablespoons butter or margarine
    Lemon wedges

Preheat oven to 500°. In a wide frying pan over medium heat, cook bacon until crisp; remove from pan, drain, crumble, and set aside. Discard all but 2 tablespoons drippings; add onion to pan and cook, stirring, until soft. Stir in bacon.

Place 2 tablespoons of the bacon-onion mixture in the cavity of each trout. Top with half a bay leaf, close cavity, and secure with a wooden or metal skewer.

In a rimmed plate or pie pan, combine crushed croutons, cheese, garlic powder, and pepper. In another rimmed plate or pie pan, beat egg with water until well combined. Dip trout in egg mixture to cover. Drain briefly; then coat completely with crumbs, shaking off excess.

Place butter on a rimmed baking sheet; set in oven for 2 to 3 minutes or until melted. Remove pan from oven. Place trout in pan and turn to coat with butter; return to oven and bake for 12 to 15 minutes or until flesh inside is just opaque when fish is prodded in thickest portion with a fork. Garnish with lemon wedges. Makes 6 servings.

Celery-stuffed Trout

Follow directions for **Bacon-stuffed Trout,** but omit bacon and bay leaves. Instead, in a wide frying pan over medium heat, melt 2 tablespoons **butter** or margarine. Add onion and cook, stirring, until soft. Add 1 cup thinly sliced **celery** and ½ teaspoon **oregano leaves;** cook, stirring, just until celery is soft. Season to taste with **salt.** Evenly divide celery mixture among trout cavities; close each cavity with a wooden or metal skewer.

Seafood Sauces

Simply cooked fish—whether grilled, baked, broiled, or poached—gets a special accent when you add a flavorful sauce. Here are three easy choices: one is delicate and buttery, one is creamy and tart, and the third is hearty with the flavors of garlic, tomatoes, and capers. Each is easy to prepare and will enhance many varieties of fish and shellfish.

Almond Browned Butter

In a medium-size frying pan over medium-high heat, melt 4 tablespoons **butter** or margarine. When butter foams, add ¼ cup sliced or slivered **almonds** and stir just until nuts begin to brown. Remove from heat and stir in 2 tablespoons **lemon juice.** Makes 4 to 6 servings.

Tartar Sauce

In a small bowl, combine ½ cup *each* **mayonnaise** and **sour cream,** 1 teaspoon **lemon juice,** ¼ cup *each* chopped **dill pickle** and chopped **green onion** (including tops), and 1 tablespoon **capers,** mashed. For a thinner sauce, add a small amount of **milk,** blending until sauce reaches desired consistency. Makes 4 to 6 servings.

Tomato-Caper Sauce

In a wide frying pan over medium heat, melt 4 tablespoons **butter** or margarine. Add 1 medium-size **onion,** chopped, and 1 clove **garlic,** minced or pressed. Cook, stirring, until onion is soft (about 5 minutes). Add 2 teaspoons **capers** and 1 can (15 oz.) **Italian-style tomatoes** (break up with a spoon) and their liquid. Cook, uncovered, stirring occasionally, until reduced and thickened (about 10 minutes). Stir in 1 tablespoon **lemon juice** and 2 tablespoons minced **parsley.** Makes 4 to 6 servings.

Fisherman's Stew

A robust, family-pleasing main dish

To complete the meal, we suggest coleslaw, hot garlic bread, and Fresh Raspberry Sundaes (page 92).

- 4 strips bacon, cut into 2-inch pieces
- 1 large onion, chopped
- 2 large thin-skinned potatoes, diced
- 1 can (about 28 oz.) Italian-style tomatoes
- 1 cup dry vermouth, or ¼ cup lemon juice plus ¾ cup water
- 1 tablespoon Worcestershire
- 4 bay leaves
- 2 or 3 cloves garlic, minced or pressed
- ½ teaspoon pepper
- 2 pounds fish fillets (ling cod, rockfish, salmon, sea bass, shark, or any combination), *each* about 1 inch thick
- Salt

In a 4 to 5-quart kettle over medium heat, cook bacon until crisp. Add onion and potatoes to bacon and drippings and cook, stirring, until onion is soft (about 10 minutes). Add tomatoes (break up with a spoon) and their liquid; stir in vermouth, Worcestershire, bay leaves, garlic, and pepper. Cover and simmer until potatoes are tender (about 30 minutes).

Meanwhile, cut fish into 2-inch pieces; add to vegetable mixture as soon as potatoes are tender, stirring gently to combine with sauce. Cover and continue cooking until flesh inside is just opaque when fish is prodded with a fork (about 5 minutes). Season to taste with salt. Makes 4 to 6 servings.

Scallop & Vegetable Pesto Sauté

A colorful mélange of well-matched flavors

To complete the meal, we suggest fluffy rice and melon wedges.

Hints for the cook: This entrée cooks quickly, so be sure to have all ingredients prepared before starting to sauté.

Any remaining pesto sauce can be stored and used later for another meal. Pour a thin layer of olive oil over sauce to prevent darkening, then cover and refrigerate for up to a week; freeze for longer storage. To use, toss with hot buttered noodles, or add to soups during the last few minutes of cooking (if frozen, do not thaw).

3 tablespoons butter or margarine
1 carrot, cut into ¼-inch slices
1 small onion, cut into 1-inch squares
1 small zucchini, cut into ¼-inch slices
8 to 10 small mushrooms, cut in half
1 small green pepper, cut into 1-inch squares
2 tablespoons thawed frozen pesto sauce, or freeze-dried pesto mix prepared according to package directions
¾ pound scallops, rinsed, drained, and cut into ¼-inch slices
Salt
Grated Parmesan cheese

In a wide frying pan over medium-high heat, melt 2 tablespoons of the butter. Add carrot and onion and cook, stirring, for 5 minutes. Add zucchini, mushrooms, and green pepper; cook, stirring, until vegetables are tender-crisp (about 5 more minutes). Remove vegetables from pan; set aside.

Add remaining 1 tablespoon butter to pan; when butter is melted, stir in pesto sauce. Add scallops and cook, stirring, until just opaque throughout when slashed (about 3 minutes). Return vegetables to pan and cook, stirring, just until heated through. Remove from heat; season to taste with salt. Sprinkle with cheese before serving. Makes 2 or 3 servings.

Scallops in Garlic Butter

Tender, juicy scallops in a flavorful butter bath

To complete the meal, we suggest crusty bread for dunking, a romaine salad, and a fruity dessert.

3 tablespoons sliced almonds
4 tablespoons butter or margarine
5 large cloves garlic, minced or pressed
2 tablespoons chopped parsley
1 teaspoon grated lemon rind
1 to 1½ pounds scallops, rinsed and drained (cut large ones in half)

Spread almonds on a baking sheet and toast in a 350° oven for about 6 minutes or until golden; set aside.

In a wide frying pan over medium heat, melt butter. Add garlic, parsley, and lemon rind and cook, stirring, for about 1 minute. Add scallops (don't crowd them in pan) and cook, turning with a wide spatula, until just opaque throughout when slashed (about 5 minutes). Transfer to a platter and top with almonds; serve immediately. Makes 4 servings.

Ginger Shrimp

A piquant sauce flavors this Chinese creation

To complete the meal, we suggest steamed rice, pineapple spears, and almond cookies.

Hint for the cook: Serve the shrimp on a bed of steamed rice; start cooking the rice before you begin to prepare the shrimp.

2 stalks celery, cut diagonally into ½-inch slices
1 can (about 8 oz.) bamboo shoots, drained
¼ cup chopped green onions (including tops)
¼ cup white wine vinegar
2 tablespoons soy sauce
5 teaspoons sugar
1 teaspoon cornstarch
3 tablespoons salad oil
2 cloves garlic, minced or pressed
2 teaspoons grated fresh ginger
1 pound medium-size shrimp, shelled and deveined
1 green onion (including top), thinly sliced

In a bowl, combine celery, bamboo shoots, and the ¼ cup onions; set aside. In another bowl, stir together vinegar, soy, sugar, and cornstarch; set aside.

Heat 2 tablespoons of the salad oil in a wok or wide frying pan over medium-high heat. When oil is hot, add garlic and ginger and stir once; then add shrimp and stir-fry until all shrimp turn pink on outside (3 to 4 minutes). Remove from pan and set aside.

Add remaining 1 tablespoon oil to pan. When oil is hot, add vegetables and stir-fry for 1 minute. Return shrimp to pan. Stir vinegar mixture once; add to pan and cook, stirring, until sauce bubbles and thickens (about 1 minute). Transfer mixture to a platter and garnish with remaining onion. Makes 3 or 4 servings.

Hangtown Fry

Cheddar melted over savory eggs and oysters

To complete the meal, we suggest hot dinner rolls and green beans vinaigrette.

>   3 tablespoons butter or margarine
>   1 jar (10 oz.) Pacific oysters, drained well and cut into bite-size pieces
>   6 eggs
>   ⅓ cup half-and-half (light cream)
>   2 tablespoons *each* finely chopped green onion (including top) and green pepper
>   ½ cup shredded sharp Cheddar cheese
>   Dash *each* of salt and pepper
>   4 strips bacon, crisply cooked, drained, and crumbled
>   Lemon wedges
>   Catsup

In a wide broiler-proof frying pan over medium heat, melt butter; add oysters and cook until edges curl (about 3 minutes). Meanwhile, in a bowl, beat eggs; add cream, onion, green pepper, 2 tablespoons of the cheese, salt, and pepper. Beat until well combined. Pour egg mixture over oysters; as edges begin to set, lift cooked portion and tilt pan to allow uncooked egg to flow underneath. Cook until eggs are almost completely set, but still moist on top.

Sprinkle eggs with bacon and remaining 6 tablespoons cheese; broil about 4 inches below heat just until cheese is bubbly. Cut into wedges and serve immediately; pass lemon wedges and catsup at the table. Makes 4 to 6 servings.

Butter-basted Crab

Hot cracked crab, simple and glorious

To complete the meal, we suggest crusty bread for dunking, a spinach-and-tomato salad, and chilled white wine.

>   4 tablespoons butter or margarine
>   ¼ teaspoon grated lemon peel
>   3 tablespoons lemon juice
>   1 tablespoon thinly sliced green onion (including top)
>   1 teaspoon *each* finely chopped parsley and soy sauce
>   Liquid hot pepper seasoning
>   1 cooked whole crab in shell (about 2 lbs.), cleaned and cracked
>   Lemon wedges

In a small pan over medium heat, melt butter; add lemon peel, lemon juice, onion, parsley, and soy. Season to taste with hot pepper seasoning. Simmer, uncovered, for 3 to 5 minutes.

Arrange crab pieces in an even layer in a 7 by 11-inch baking dish. Brush butter mixture over crab and bake, covered, in a 300° oven for about 20 minutes (basting often with pan juices) or until heated through. Garnish with lemon wedges; provide nutcrackers and small forks for removing meat from shells. Makes 2 servings.

Savory Steamed Clams

Whole clams in a thyme-scented rice broth

Pictured on facing page

To complete the meal, we suggest tossed green salad, crusty bread, and cold beer.

>   ¾ cup long grain white rice
>   2 tablespoons olive oil or salad oil
>   1 large onion, chopped
>   2 cloves garlic, minced or pressed
>   1 bay leaf
>   ½ teaspoon thyme leaves
>   3 tablespoons chopped parsley
>   1 cup dry white wine or regular-strength chicken broth
>   1 bottle (8 oz.) clam juice
>   20 to 30 small live hard-shell clams, scrubbed well
>   2 tomatoes, seeded and chopped

In a small pan, cook rice according to package directions. Meanwhile, heat oil in a 5 to 6-quart kettle over medium heat. Add onion and garlic and cook, stirring, until onion is soft. Stir in bay leaf, thyme, parsley, wine, and clam juice. Cover, reduce heat, and simmer for 5 minutes.

Add clams; cover and simmer until clams open (10 to 12 minutes). Discard any unopened clams. Stir in tomatoes and rice; cover and cook until heated through. Ladle clams and broth into individual bowls. Makes 3 or 4 servings.

Some call them steamers. The Italians call them *vongole*. To others, they're just plain clams. Whatever you label them, these succulent bivalves are simply delicious—especially when served in a savory broth. The recipe is on this page.

Poultry

For greater efficiency:

Purchase poultry carefully. Choose plump birds with well-rounded breasts and smooth un-bruised skin. Skin color is not an indication of quality; it will vary from yellow to bluish white depending on what the bird was fed. In selecting prepackaged poultry, look for packages with little or no liquid in the bottom.

Store uncooked poultry properly. Fresh poultry is perishable and should be cooked within 2 days; in the meantime, store it, covered with plastic wrap, in the coldest part of your refrigerator. Before you refrigerate whole birds, remove the giblets. Freeze the heart and gizzard in one container and the liver in another; collect more of each until you accumulate enough for a meal or other purposes. If you're using frozen poultry, remove it from the freezer a day in advance and thaw in the refrigerator.

Roast two chickens at once. If you're planning a roast chicken dinner, cook two birds instead of one. Slice the second bird for sandwich meat, or cut it into pieces to use in Curried Chicken (page 72) or in main-dish salads (pages 20, 21).

One 3 to 3½-pound frying chicken will yield 3 cups of diced cooked meat.

Broil instead of barbecuing. Broiling and barbecuing are similar techniques; both use direct, dry heat as a method of cooking. But if you don't have time to start up the barbecue, broil poultry instead—you'll cut cooking time in half. Place poultry (halves, quarters, or pieces) on a greased rack in a broiler pan; then broil 6 inches below heat for just 20 minutes (turn after 10 minutes).

Cook chicken breasts in a microwave. When a recipe calls for diced cooked chicken and you don't have any leftover poultry, use your microwave oven to cook chicken breasts. One large whole chicken breast (1 lb.) will yield about 1½ cups of diced cooked meat. Split chicken breasts in half lengthwise and place, skin side up, on a large plate. Cover with wax paper and microwave on high for 4 to 5 minutes per pound; then let stand, covered, for 5 minutes. When chicken is done, meat in thickest part will no longer be pink when slashed.

Oven-sautéed Garlic Chicken

Garlic and onions make hearty partners for chicken

To complete the meal, we suggest buttered spaghetti, Brussels sprouts, and iceberg lettuce wedges with a creamy dressing.

    4 tablespoons butter or margarine
    1 large onion, thinly sliced and separated
      into rings
    6 to 8 chicken pieces (breasts, legs, or thighs) or
      1 frying chicken, cut into pieces (about 3 lbs.
      total)
    2 teaspoons paprika
    1 teaspoon salt
    ¼ cup *each* catsup and dry white wine
    6 cloves garlic, peeled

Place butter in a 10 by 15-inch rimmed baking pan; set in oven while it preheats to 425°. When butter is melted, scatter onion rings over bottom of pan. Brush chicken pieces with a little of the melted butter; arrange over onions. Sprinkle chicken with paprika and salt.

In a small bowl, stir together catsup and wine; carefully pour into pan (but not directly over chicken pieces). Tuck garlic cloves among chicken pieces.

Bake, covered, in a 425° oven for 30 minutes. Uncover and bake for 15 more minutes or until meat near thighbone (or in thickest part of breasts, if using all breasts) is no longer pink when slashed. Discard garlic and serve chicken with pan juices. Makes 4 to 6 servings.

Honey Citrus Chicken

Sweetly glazed chicken with orange slices

To complete the meal, we suggest buttered peas or sautéed zucchini rounds, bran muffins, and tall glasses of iced tea.

    1 frying chicken (3 to 3½ lbs.), cut into pieces
    ⅓ cup honey
    2 teaspoons *each* grated lemon peel and
      orange peel
    ¼ cup lemon juice
    1½ teaspoons Dijon mustard
    ½ teaspoon curry powder
    ½ teaspoon ground ginger or 1 teaspoon grated
      fresh ginger
    1 large orange, unpeeled

Arrange chicken, skin side down, in a greased 10 by 15-inch rimmed baking pan. In a bowl, stir together honey, lemon peel, orange peel, lemon juice, mustard, curry powder, and ginger. Brush half of honey mixture over chicken pieces.

Cut orange in half lengthwise, then cut crosswise into ¼-inch slices. Tuck orange slices around chicken.

Bake, uncovered, in a 375° oven for 30 minutes; then turn chicken pieces over and brush with remaining honey mixture. Bake for 20 more minutes or until meat near thighbone is no longer pink when slashed. Serve with orange slices and pan juices. Makes 4 servings.

Tandoori Chicken

A spicy dish featuring the flavors of India

To complete the meal, we suggest sautéed onions, rice pilaf, melon wedges, and hot tea.

    2 teaspoons *each* grated fresh ginger and
      ground allspice
    ½ teaspoon crushed red pepper
    3 cloves garlic, minced or pressed
    2 tablespoons lemon juice
    6 large chicken legs with thighs attached (3 to
      3½ lbs. *total*)
      Plain yogurt

Stir together ginger, allspice, red pepper, garlic, and lemon juice to form a paste. Loosen skin of each thigh by slipping your fingers between skin and flesh; also loosen skin over leg-thigh joint. Spread ½ teaspoon of the paste over flesh of each leg and thigh. Spread remaining paste over all skin surfaces.

Place chicken pieces, skin side down, on a greased rack in a broiler pan. Broil about 6 inches below heat for 10 minutes. Turn pieces over and continue to broil until meat near thighbone is no longer pink when slashed (about 10 more minutes). Transfer chicken to a heated platter and serve immediately; accompany with cold yogurt to spoon over individual servings. Makes 6 servings.

Tarragon Chicken with Vegetables

Chicken and vegetables broil side by side

Pictured on facing page and on front cover

To complete the meal, we suggest crusty rolls and white wine.

Hint for the cook: Vary vegetables according to the season or your preference. Two flavorful options are tomato halves and green onions.

> 6 tablespoons butter or margarine, softened
> 2 large cloves garlic, minced or pressed
> 1 teaspoon dry tarragon
> ½ teaspoon pepper
> 1 frying chicken (3 to 3½ lbs.), split lengthwise
> 4 to 6 large mushrooms
> 4 *each* small zucchini and crookneck squash, cut in half lengthwise
> 1 green or red bell pepper, cut into quarters and seeded

In a small bowl, blend butter with garlic, tarragon, and pepper. Loosen chicken skin by slipping your fingers under it, starting at top of breast and back. Using about 1 tablespoon for each chicken half, rub a thin layer of herb butter between skin and flesh. Rub another ½ tablespoon herb butter over cut side of each half. In a small pan, melt remaining 3 tablespoons herb butter; set aside.

Place chicken halves, skin side down, on a greased rack in a broiler pan. Broil about 6 inches below heat for 20 minutes; brush with reserved herb butter after 10 minutes. Turn chicken over and arrange vegetables alongside. Brush chicken and vegetables with remaining herb butter.

Continue to broil until meat near thighbone is no longer pink when slashed (15 to 20 more minutes). Cut each half in half. Arrange chicken quarters on a platter; arrange vegetables around chicken. Makes 4 servings.

Chili-glazed Chicken with Vegetables

Prepare **Tarragon Chicken,** but in preparing the herb butter, substitute 1 teaspoon **chili powder** for the dry tarragon and add 2 tablespoons **lime juice** and ¼ teaspoon *each* **ground cumin** and grated **lime peel.**

Cheerful garden colors make Tarragon Chicken with Vegetables (recipe on this page) a good choice for a festive dinner. Another part of the fun: creative cooks can vary the vegetables as they please.

Baked Chutney Chicken

Glossy with tangy-sweet chutney

To complete the meal, we suggest rice, a tossed green salad, and ice cream sundaes.

> 1 frying chicken (3 to 3½ lbs.), cut into pieces
> ⅓ cup *each* soy sauce and finely chopped Major Grey chutney
> Parsley sprigs

Place chicken pieces in a 9 by 13-inch baking dish. Pour soy over chicken and let marinate for 15 minutes, turning often. Drain soy from dish and discard. Arrange chicken pieces, skin side up, in a single layer; brush evenly with chutney.

Bake, uncovered, in a 350° oven for 45 minutes or until meat near thighbone is no longer pink when slashed. Arrange chicken on a platter; garnish with parsley sprigs. Makes 4 servings.

Orange Chicken with Carrots

Orange juice flavors both chicken and carrots

To complete the meal, we suggest buttered noodles, a crisp green salad, and brownies.

> 1 frying chicken (3 to 3½ lbs.), cut into pieces and skinned
> 5 or 6 medium-size carrots, cut diagonally into ½-inch slices
> 1 can (6 oz.) frozen orange juice concentrate, thawed
> 2 tablespoons cornstarch
> ½ teaspoon salt
> ⅛ teaspoon white pepper
> ¼ cup chopped green onions (including tops)

Arrange chicken (place breasts bony side down) in a 9 by 13-inch baking dish; scatter carrots over top. Combine orange juice concentrate, cornstarch, salt, and pepper; spoon over carrots and chicken.

Bake, covered, in a 375° oven for 40 minutes. Remove from oven and baste with pan juices; sprinkle with onions. Cover again and return to oven for 15 more minutes or until meat near thighbone is no longer pink when slashed. Makes 4 servings.

Harvest Chicken with Roasted Vegetables

A one-pan oven entrée

To complete the meal, we suggest bread sticks, chilled wine, and fresh strawberries.

Hint for the cook: If you have extra time, you can use a whole frying chicken (3½ to 4 lbs.) instead of chicken legs; roast for 1 to 1¼ hours.

> 4 to 8 thin-skinned potatoes, *each* 2 to 3 inches in diameter
> 2 tablespoons butter or margarine
> 4 large chicken legs with thighs attached (3 to 3½ lbs. *total*)
> 3 large carrots, cut into 1½-inch chunks
> 4 small pattypan squash
> 3 medium-size crookneck squash, cut into 1½-inch chunks
> 2 large green or red bell peppers, seeded and quartered
> 2 cloves garlic, quartered
> 1 large onion, quartered
> 8 cherry tomatoes
> 3 sprigs (*each* about 2 inches long) fresh rosemary or 1 teaspoon dry rosemary

Pierce potatoes in several places and set on oven rack as oven preheats to 375°. Spread butter over bottom of a 12 by 15-inch rimmed baking pan. Place chicken pieces, skin side down, in pan.

Arrange carrots, pattypan squash (leave whole), crookneck squash, peppers, garlic, onion, and tomatoes around chicken pieces. Place rosemary sprigs on vegetables (or sprinkle vegetables with dry rosemary).

Roast, uncovered, in oven with potatoes for 45 minutes or until meat near thighbone is no longer pink when slashed and potatoes feel soft when squeezed. Stir vegetables occasionally while roasting.

Transfer chicken to a large platter; carefully lift vegetables from pan with a slotted spoon and mound alongside chicken. Spoon pan juices over vegetables; serve potatoes separately. Makes 4 servings.

Crisp Broil-Bake Chicken

Juicy and tender meat, crisp skin

To complete the meal, we suggest corn on the cob, cole slaw, and melon wedges.

> 1 frying chicken, cut into pieces, or 6 legs with thighs attached (3 to 3½ lbs. *total*)
> Salt and pepper
> Garlic powder
> 1 teaspoon thyme leaves
> Boiling water

Lightly sprinkle both sides of chicken pieces with salt, pepper, and garlic powder; then arrange skin side down, not touching, on a greased rack in a broiler pan. Broil about 6 inches below heat until chicken is lightly browned (about 10 minutes).

Remove broiler pan from oven, adjust oven rack to center of oven, and reset oven to 500°. Turn chicken pieces over and sprinkle with thyme. Set pan back in oven; pour boiling water into pan under chicken to a depth of ½ inch.

Bake for 20 to 25 minutes or until chicken is browned and meat near thighbone is no longer pink when slashed. Makes 4 to 6 servings.

Curry-spiced Broil-Bake Chicken

Follow directions for **Crisp Broil-Bake Chicken** but omit thyme leaves. In a bowl, combine 2 teaspoons **curry powder,** 1 teaspoon **oregano leaves,** ½ teaspoon *each* **dry mustard** and **garlic powder,** and ¼ teaspoon **paprika;** before broiling, sprinkle chicken pieces with half the curry mixture. After turning chicken pieces over on rack, sprinkle with remaining mixture.

Swiss Chicken

Blanketed with cream sauce and cheese

To complete the meal, we suggest buttered noodles and green beans.

> 1 tablespoon butter or margarine
> 1 tablespoon salad oil
> 2 large whole chicken breasts (about 2 lbs. *total*), split, skinned, and boned
> ¼ cup dry sherry
> ¼ teaspoon salt
> ½ teaspoon paprika
> ⅔ cup whipping cream
> ½ cup shredded Swiss cheese

Melt butter in oil in a wide frying pan over medium-high heat. When butter mixture sizzles, add chicken breasts and cook until golden on the outside and no longer pink inside when slashed in thickest part (5 to 7 minutes on each side). Lift out chicken and arrange on an ovenproof platter; keep warm.

Stir sherry into pan; add salt, paprika, and cream. Bring to a boil; then boil until surface is covered with large, shiny bubbles and sauce is reduced to ½ cup. Pour sauce over breasts, sprinkle with cheese, and broil 6 inches below heat just until cheese is melted. Makes 4 servings.

Salsa Chicken with Cheese

Colorful, chile-spiced, and cheesy

To complete the meal, we suggest warm buttered tortillas, avocado and orange salad, and beer.

- 2 tablespoons butter or margarine
- 2 tablespoons salad oil
- 3 whole chicken breasts (about 3 lbs. *total*), split, skinned, and boned
- 1 medium-size onion, chopped
- 1 clove garlic, minced or pressed
- 2 stalks celery, thinly sliced
- 1 can (4 oz.) diced green chiles
- 1 can (1 lb.) stewed tomatoes
- ¼ teaspoon ground cumin
- ½ teaspoon oregano leaves
  Salt and pepper
- 1½ cups (6 oz.) shredded Cheddar cheese

Melt butter in oil in a wide frying pan over medium-high heat. When butter mixture sizzles, add chicken breasts and cook until golden (about 5 minutes on each side). Remove breasts and set aside; keep warm.

Add onion, garlic, and celery to pan drippings; cook until vegetables are soft (about 5 minutes). Stir in chiles, tomatoes (break up with a spoon) and their liquid, cumin, and oregano. Cook, uncovered, over medium-high heat, stirring occasionally, until slightly thickened (about 10 minutes). Add chicken breasts and continue to cook, covered, until meat in thickest part is no longer pink when slashed (about 5 more minutes).

Season to taste with salt and pepper; then arrange chicken breasts on an ovenproof platter. Spoon sauce over breasts, sprinkle with cheese, and broil 6 inches below heat just until cheese is melted. Makes 6 servings.

Kung Pao Chicken

Fiery red chiles season this Chinese specialty

To complete the meal, we suggest rice, steamed Chinese pea pods, and a fruit compote.

Hint for the cook: Watch the chiles closely as they cook—don't allow them to burn. Burned chiles release potent volatile oils that sting the nose and eyes.

- 1 tablespoon *each* dry sherry and cornstarch
- ½ teaspoon salt
- ⅛ teaspoon white pepper
- 1½ pounds chicken breasts, split, skinned, boned, and cut into bite-size pieces
- 4 tablespoons salad oil
  Cooking Sauce (recipe follows)
- 4 to 6 small dried whole hot red chiles
- ½ cup salted peanuts
- 1 teaspoon *each* minced garlic and grated fresh ginger
- 2 whole green onions (including tops), cut into 1½-inch lengths

In a bowl, combine sherry, cornstarch, salt, and pepper. Add chicken and stir to coat, then stir in 1 tablespoon of the oil and let marinate for 15 minutes. Prepare Cooking Sauce and set aside.

Heat a wok or wide frying pan over medium heat. When pan is hot, add 1 tablespoon of the oil. Add chiles and peanuts and cook, stirring, until chiles just begin to char. (If chiles become completely black, discard them. Remove peanuts from pan and set aside; repeat with new oil and chiles.) Remove peanuts and chiles from pan; discard chiles and set peanuts aside.

Add remaining 2 tablespoons oil to pan and increase heat to high. When oil begins to heat, add garlic and ginger. Stir once, then add chicken and stir-fry until chicken is opaque (about 3 minutes); then add peanuts and onions. Stir Cooking Sauce and pour into pan; cook, stirring, until sauce boils and thickens. Makes 4 servings.

Cooking Sauce. In a bowl, combine 2 tablespoons **soy sauce,** 1 tablespoon *each* **white wine vinegar** and **dry sherry,** 3 tablespoons regular-strength **chicken broth** or water, and 2 teaspoons *each* **sugar** and **cornstarch.**

Chicken & Apple Sauté

Subtly sweet with sherry and apples

Pictured on facing page

To complete the meal, we suggest a butter lettuce salad, steamed broccoli or asparagus spears, and white wine.

Hint for the cook: Choose firm-textured tart apples such as Newtown pippin, Gravenstein, Jonathan, or Granny Smith; to prevent apples from darkening, slice them just before using.

> 4 tablespoons butter or margarine
> 2 large tart apples, cored and cut into ¼-inch slices
> 2 large whole chicken breasts (about 2 lbs. *total*), split and boned
> 1 large onion, chopped
> ⅔ cup dry sherry or apple juice
> ⅓ cup whipping cream
>   Watercress (optional)

In a wide frying pan over medium heat, melt 2 tablespoons of the butter. Add apple slices; cook, stirring frequently, just until tender (1 to 2 minutes). Set aside and keep warm.

Increase heat to medium-high; add remaining 2 tablespoons butter to pan. When butter sizzles, add chicken breasts, skin side down, and cook until golden (about 5 minutes on each side); remove from pan, set aside, and keep warm.

Add onion to pan juices and cook, stirring occasionally, until golden (about 5 minutes); add sherry and cook for 1 minute. Return chicken to pan, skin side up. Cover, reduce heat, and simmer until meat in thickest part is no longer pink when slashed (about 5 minutes).

Arrange chicken breasts on a platter; top with apple slices. Stir cream into pan juices and increase heat to high. Bring to a boil; then boil, uncovered, until surface is covered with large, shiny bubbles and sauce is reduced by one-third. Pour sauce over chicken. Garnish with watercress, if desired. Makes 4 servings.

Chicken & Mushroom Sauté

Prepare **Chicken & Apple Sauté,** but substitute ¼ pound **mushrooms,** sliced, for the apples. Use sherry or a dry white wine, and eliminate cream. After transferring chicken to platter, increase heat and boil sauce, uncovered, until reduced by half.

Cashew Chicken

Chicken morsels stir-fried with vegetables and nuts

To complete the meal, we suggest steamed bok choy or spinach, and rolls or rice.

Hints for the cook: You can substitute walnut halves, almonds, or peanuts for the cashews. Vary the vegetables according to the season or your preference.

> **Cooking Sauce** (recipe follows)
> 1 whole chicken breast (about 1 lb.), split, skinned, boned, and cut into bite-size pieces
> 1 tablespoon soy sauce
> 1 teaspoon cornstarch
> 3 tablespoons salad oil
> ½ cup salted cashews
> 1 medium-size green pepper, seeded and cut into 1-inch squares
> 1 medium-size onion, cut into 8 wedges and separated into layers
> ½ teaspoon finely minced fresh ginger or ¼ teaspoon ground ginger

Prepare Cooking Sauce; set aside. Mix chicken with soy and cornstarch; set aside.

Heat a wok or wide frying pan over medium-high heat. When pan is hot, add 2 tablespoons of the oil. Add cashews and stir-fry until browned (about 1 minute). Remove with a slotted spoon and set aside. Add chicken and stir-fry until opaque (about 3 minutes); remove from pan and set aside.

Add remaining 1 tablespoon oil to pan; then add green pepper, onion, and ginger and stir-fry until pepper is tender-crisp (about 1 minute). Return chicken to pan. Stir Cooking Sauce and pour into pan; stir-fry until sauce bubbles and thickens. Stir in cashews. Makes 2 servings.

Cooking Sauce. In a bowl, combine ½ teaspoon **cornstarch,** dash of **liquid hot pepper seasoning,** ¾ teaspoon *each* **sugar** and **white wine vinegar,** 1 teaspoon **dry sherry** or water, and 1 tablespoon **soy sauce.**

Serve up some elegance with Chicken & Apple Sauté (recipe on this page). Perfect for last-minute entertaining, it's a quickly prepared entrée of tender boned chicken breasts, buttery sautéed apple slices, sherry, and a kiss of cream.

Curried Chicken

Chunks of chicken in a curry-spiced gravy

To complete the meal, we suggest broiled tomato halves, rice, and sherbet.

> **Condiments: Shredded coconut, sliced bananas (coated with lemon juice to prevent browning), diced cucumber, raisins, peanuts, chutney, plain yogurt, chopped hard-cooked egg**
>
> 4 **tablespoons butter or margarine**
> 1 **large onion, chopped**
> 3 **tablespoons all-purpose flour**
> 2 to 3 **teaspoons curry powder**
> 2 **teaspoons sugar**
> ½ **teaspoon ground ginger**
> 1 **can (14½ oz.) regular-strength chicken broth**
> 1 **cup milk**
> 1 **teaspoon lemon juice**
> 3 **cups diced cooked chicken, turkey, lamb, or beef; or 1 pound small cooked shrimp**

Prepare 4 or more of the condiments, placing each item selected in an individual bowl; set aside.

In a wide frying pan over medium heat, melt butter; add onion and cook until soft. Stir in flour, curry powder, sugar, and ginger; cook until bubbly. Remove pan from heat. Gradually stir in broth. Return pan to heat and cook, stirring, until sauce is thickened. Stir in milk, lemon juice, and chicken; cook, stirring, until heated through (about 5 minutes).

At the table, pass condiments to sprinkle over individual servings. Makes 4 servings.

Chicken Tostadas

A whole meal built atop a crisp-fried tortilla

To complete the meal, we suggest carrot sticks, Mexican beer or iced tea, and caramel custard.

> **Tomato Salsa (recipe follows)**
> **Salad oil**
> 4 **corn tortillas**
> 1 **can (8 oz.) refried beans**
> 1 **cup (4 oz.) shredded jack or Cheddar cheese**
> 1 **quart shredded, lightly packed iceberg lettuce**
> 1 to 2 **cups shredded cooked chicken or turkey**
> **Avocado slices or guacamole**
> **Sour cream**

Prepare Tomato Salsa and set aside. Pour salad oil into a 7-inch frying pan to a depth of ½ inch; heat over medium-high heat. When oil is hot, add 1 tortilla to pan; fry until crisp, slightly puffed, and lightly browned (about 1 minute or less), using a spatula or tongs to turn tortilla frequently or hold it under oil. Drain on paper towels. Repeat with remaining 3 tortillas; place each tortilla on a plate.

Meanwhile, place beans in a small pan and cook over medium heat, stirring occasionally, just until heated through. Spread each tortilla with ¼ of the beans and sprinkle with ¼ of the cheese. Place 1 cup lettuce atop each tortilla; then top with ¼ of the chicken pieces. Drizzle some of the salsa over chicken; top with avocado slices and a dollop of sour cream. Pass remaining salsa at the table to spoon over individual servings. Makes 4 servings.

Tomato Salsa. Peel, seed, and finely chop 3 medium-size **tomatoes;** place in a small bowl. Finely chop 3 **green onions** (including tops) and stir into tomatoes, along with ¼ cup diced **green chiles,** 2 tablespoons chopped fresh **coriander** (cilantro), ½ teaspoon **salt,** and 1 tablespoon **olive oil.**

Chicken Divan

Velvety cheese sauce tops broccoli and chicken

To complete the meal, we suggest a tomato vinaigrette salad, and rolls or bread sticks.

> 1 **package (about 10 oz.) frozen broccoli spears or chopped broccoli**
> 3 **cups shredded cooked chicken or turkey**
> 3 **tablespoons butter or margarine**
> 3 **tablespoons all-purpose flour**
> ¾ **teaspoon dry mustard**
> 1½ **cups milk**
> 1½ **cups (6 oz.) shredded sharp Cheddar cheese**
> **Salt and pepper**
> **Paprika**

Cook broccoli according to package directions; drain thoroughly. Spread broccoli evenly in a greased 7 by 11-inch baking dish. Evenly distribute chicken over broccoli; set aside.

In a 1 to 1½-quart pan over medium heat, melt butter. Add flour and mustard and cook, stirring, until bubbly (about 1 minute). Remove from heat and gradually stir in milk. Return pan to heat and cook, stirring, until sauce is smooth, thick, and boiling. Remove from heat; add 1 cup of the cheese. Stir until cheese is melted, then season to taste with salt and pepper. Pour sauce over chicken. Sprinkle remaining ½ cup cheese over sauce, then sprinkle with paprika.

Bake, uncovered, in a 350° oven for about 30 minutes or until heated through and cheese sauce is bubbly. Makes 4 servings.

Italian Roast Game Hens & Potatoes

Buttery roast potato spears complement the hens

To complete the meal, we suggest sautéed red or green bell peppers, and a tossed green salad.

- ½ cup (¼ lb.) butter or margarine
- ¼ teaspoon *each* paprika, oregano leaves, and thyme leaves
- 2 Rock Cornish game hens (about 24 oz. *each*), split lengthwise
- 2 large russet potatoes, scrubbed
  Cherry tomatoes

In a 1-quart pan over medium heat, melt butter with paprika, oregano, and thyme. Brush about 1 tablespoon of the herb butter over cut surface of each hen half; then place halves, skin side up, in a 9 by 13-inch baking pan (not on a rack). Brush another 2 tablespoons herb butter over hens.

Cut potatoes in half lengthwise; then cut each half lengthwise into four wedges. Brush cut surfaces of potatoes with remaining 4 tablespoons herb butter. Place potatoes, skin side down, in a 9-inch square baking pan.

Place pans side by side in a 450° oven. Bake, uncovered, for 30 to 35 minutes or until meat near thighbone is no longer pink when slashed and potatoes are fork-tender. Arrange hen halves on a platter; surround with potato wedges and cherry tomatoes. Makes 4 servings.

French Roast Game Hens & Potatoes

Follow directions for **Italian Roast Game Hens & Potatoes** but omit paprika, oregano leaves, and thyme leaves. Add 1 tablespoon finely minced **onion** to melted butter and cook for 5 minutes or until onion is soft. Stir in ¼ teaspoon *each* **dry mustard, fines herbes,** and **garlic powder,** and a dash of **liquid hot pepper seasoning.**

Chicken Liver & Mushroom Sauté

Creamy chicken livers perch atop English muffins

To complete the meal, we suggest sliced tomato and cucumber salad, or a fresh fruit cup.

- 3 tablespoons butter or margarine
- ¾ pound chicken livers, cut in half
- ¼ pound mushrooms, quartered
- 1½ teaspoons all-purpose flour
- ¼ teaspoon *each* fines herbes and salt
- 2 tablespoons dry sherry
- ¼ cup regular-strength chicken broth
- 2 English muffins, split and toasted
  Chopped parsley

In a wide frying pan over medium-high heat, melt butter. Add livers and mushrooms and cook, stirring occasionally, just until livers are browned (about 5 minutes). Stir in flour, fines herbes, and salt; remove from heat and gradually stir in sherry and broth. Return to heat and cook, stirring, until sauce is thickened (about 3 minutes).

Place 2 muffin halves, toasted side up, on each of 2 plates. Spoon chicken liver mixture over muffin halves; sprinkle with parsley. Makes 2 servings.

Chicken Livers & Onions

Sweet cooked onions with sautéed chicken livers

To complete the meal, we suggest mashed potatoes, Broccoli Polonaise (page 52), and white wine.

- 4 tablespoons butter or margarine
- 2 large onions, thinly sliced and separated into rings
- 1 pound chicken livers, cut in half
- ½ teaspoon dry rosemary
  Salt and pepper

In a wide frying pan over medium heat, melt butter. Add onions and cook, stirring occasionally, until golden (15 to 20 minutes). With a slotted spoon, transfer onions to a plate; reserve pan juices. Increase heat to medium-high and add chicken livers. Cook, stirring often, until livers are just firm but still slightly pink in center when slashed (about 5 minutes). Add onions and rosemary to pan; cook and stir until onions are heated through (about 1 minute). Season to taste with salt and pepper. Makes 3 or 4 servings.

Minced Turkey in Lettuce

A piquant mélange wrapped in lettuce leaves

Pictured on facing page

To complete the meal, we suggest fresh grapes, hot tea, and Chinese cookies.

Hints for the cook: Have all ingredients assembled before starting to stir-fry.

If you have time, cut the 1½-inch lengths of green onion into decorative brushes by thinly slicing at both ends, then dropping into ice water for 5 minutes to curl. Use a few to garnish the hoisin sauce.

Cooking Sauce (recipe follows)
4 tablespoons salad oil
2 large cloves garlic, minced or pressed
1 teaspoon grated fresh ginger
¼ to ½ teaspoon crushed red pepper
1 pound ground turkey, or 1½ pounds chicken breasts, split, skinned, boned, and minced
1 can (8 oz.) bamboo shoots, minced
1 can (8 oz.) water chestnuts, minced
¼ pound mushrooms, minced
4 green onions (including tops), minced
½ cup frozen peas
Hoisin sauce (optional)
Chilled butter lettuce or romaine leaves
2 green onions (green part only), cut into 1½-inch lengths

Prepare Cooking Sauce and set aside. Heat a wok or wide frying pan over high heat. When pan is hot, add 2 tablespoons of the oil; then add garlic, ginger, and red pepper and stir once. Add turkey and stir-fry, breaking up large chunks, until opaque (about 3 minutes); remove from pan and set aside.

Add remaining 2 tablespoons oil to pan. When oil is hot, add bamboo shoots, water chestnuts, mushrooms, and onions; stir-fry for 2 minutes. Return turkey to pan along with peas. Stir Cooking Sauce, pour into pan, and cook, stirring, until sauce boils and thickens. Serve immediately.

To eat, spread a little hoisin (if used) on a lettuce leaf. Place a piece of green onion on top, spoon in some turkey mixture, then wrap up and eat out of hand. Makes 4 to 6 servings.

Cooking Sauce. In a bowl, combine 2 teaspoons **cornstarch,** 1 tablespoon **dry sherry,** 2 tablespoons *each* **soy sauce** and **water,** and ½ teaspoon **sugar.**

Turkey-Bacon Logs

Bacon strips swirled around logs of ground turkey

To complete the meal, we suggest dinner rolls and crisp stir-fried vegetables.

Hint for the cook: If you can't purchase ground turkey in your local market, you can use a food processor to make your own. Cut 1 pound raw boned turkey meat (use a leg or small breast half) into 1-inch chunks. Divide turkey pieces into 3 portions; process, one portion at a time, using 3 long bursts for each portion, until finely chopped.

1 egg
¼ cup fine dry bread crumbs
¼ teaspoon *each* salt and white pepper
1 pound ground turkey
¼ cup *each* minced parsley and chopped green onions (including tops)
8 strips bacon
Cranberry Sauce (recipe follows)

Beat egg in a bowl; stir in bread crumbs, salt, and pepper and let stand for 1 minute. Add turkey, parsley, and onions; mix lightly until well combined. Divide mixture into 8 equal portions and shape each into a 3½-inch-long log. Wrap a strip of bacon spiral-fashion around each log, securing ends of each strip with a wooden pick.

Place logs on a greased rack in a baking pan. Bake, uncovered, in a 450° oven for 20 minutes or until turkey meat is no longer pink when slashed. Meanwhile, prepare Cranberry Sauce; place in a serving bowl to pass at the table. Remove picks from logs before serving. Makes 4 servings.

Cranberry Sauce. In a 1-quart pan, stir together 1 can (8 oz.) **whole-berry cranberry sauce,** 3 tablespoons *each* **sugar** and **water,** ½ cup **golden raisins,** ¼ teaspoon *each* **ground cinnamon** and grated **lemon peel,** 1 tablespoon **lemon juice,** and ⅛ teaspoon **ground cloves.** Cook over medium heat, stirring occasionally, for 10 minutes or until heated through.

No chopsticks are required for Minced Turkey in Lettuce (recipe on this page). To eat this Chinese-style treat, you spoon the turkey mixture into chilled lettuce leaves, then wrap them up and eat out of hand.

Meats

For greater efficiency:

Choose quick-cooking meat cuts. The least exercised parts of any animal (such as the middle of the back, called the loin) are the most tender and should be cooked quickly. The loin portion of a steer yields porterhouse and T-bone steaks; the same portion of a lamb, pig, or calf produces lamb chops, pork chops, or veal loin chops.

You can also quick-cook less tender cuts, such as those from the round, flank, and chuck, but you'll need to tenderize the meat first. One method (generally done in the market) involves breaking down the meat's muscle fibers mechanically, either in a tenderizing machine or by grinding. You can achieve a similar result at home by pounding the meat into thin slices with a heavy, flat mallet. Or tenderize meat in a marinade of wine, vinegar, or citrus juice.

Use appropriate cooking methods. The quickest way to cook meat is with dry heat—by roasting, broiling, grilling, pan-broiling, or frying. Use tender cuts (from the loin or rib) and those that have been tenderized.

Cuts that have simply been marinated can also be cooked using dry heat. Cook them rare or medium-rare; they'll be pink and juicy. Don't cook until well done—you'll end up with dry, stringy meat.

Buy the right amount. Though appetites vary, you'll usually be safe if you allow ¼ to ⅓ pound for a serving of lean, boneless meat with little or no fat, such as ground meat, flank steak, and filets. For steaks and chops—meat with a medium amount of bone and some edge fat—allow about ½ pound per serving. For very bony cuts—prime rib bones, for instance—allow 1 full pound per serving.

Plan ahead for leftovers. When time permits, cook a larger cut of meat—one that will yield more than enough for one meal. The leftover meat can provide a thrifty, quick entrée another night. Roasted beef, lamb, or veal can be sliced and quickly reheated (see Skillet Grill, page 90); or use it in hot or cold sandwiches, stir-fry dishes, or with eggs in a frittata or omelet.

Broiled Flank Steak

Simple and succulent

To complete the meal, we suggest Broccoli Polonaise (page 52), hot rolls, and Cream Sundaes (page 92).

> 1 clove garlic, minced or pressed
> ⅓ cup salad oil
> 3 tablespoons red wine vinegar
> 2 teaspoons *each* Worcestershire, soy sauce, and dry mustard
> ¼ teaspoon pepper
>   Few drops of liquid hot pepper seasoning
> 1 flank steak (1 to 1½ lbs.)

In a shallow dish, mix garlic, oil, vinegar, Worcestershire, soy, mustard, pepper, and hot pepper seasoning. Place steak in dish; turn to coat with marinade. Let stand for 30 minutes; turn over several times.

Remove steak from marinade; drain briefly, reserving marinade. Place steak on a lightly greased rack in a broiler pan. Broil about 4 inches below heat until done to your liking when slashed (3 to 4 minutes on each side for rare). Baste with reserved marinade several times during cooking.

Transfer steak to a carving board and cut across the grain into thin slanting slices. Makes 4 to 6 servings.

Savory Sirloin Steak

Herbed butter gives a flourish to thick steak

To complete the meal, we suggest Broiled Tomatoes Parmesan (page 53), buttered green beans, and rolls.

> 3 tablespoons butter or margarine, softened
> 2 large cloves garlic, minced or pressed
> ½ teaspoon *each* dry basil and pepper
> ¼ teaspoon salt
> 2 tablespoons fine dry bread crumbs
> 1 top sirloin beef steak (1½ to 2 lbs.), cut 1¼ inches thick

In a small bowl, blend butter, garlic, basil, pepper, salt, and bread crumbs; set aside. Place steak on a greased rack in a broiler pan. Roast in a 500° oven for 12 to 15 minutes for rare, or until done to your liking when slashed. Remove pan from oven and turn on broiler.

Press butter mixture evenly over top of steak;

broil 3 inches below heat until butter mixture is melted and bubbly (about 3 minutes). Transfer steak to a carving board and cut across the grain into thin slanting slices. Makes 4 to 6 servings.

Stir-fry Beef

Oriental flavors accent this meaty mélange

To complete the meal, we suggest fresh fruits of the season, fortune cookies, and a pot of tea.

Hint for the cook: If you prefer, you can serve the beef on a bed of steamed rice, instead of over hot cooked spinach.

> About 1 pound beef top round or sirloin tip
> ¼ cup dry red wine
> 2 tablespoons soy sauce
> 1 clove garlic, minced or pressed
> 1 teaspoon minced fresh ginger
> 2 tablespoons salad oil
> 1 cup thinly sliced celery
> 1 medium-size red or green bell pepper, seeded and cut into 1-inch squares
> 1 can (8 oz.) water chestnuts, drained and sliced
> ½ cup thinly sliced green onions (including tops)
> 2 tablespoons hoisin sauce
>   Hot cooked fresh or frozen spinach

Slice meat into thin strips and place in a shallow dish. Stir together wine, soy, garlic, and ginger; pour over meat and let stand for about 30 minutes.

Heat oil in a wok or wide frying pan over high heat; add meat and marinade and stir-fry for 2 to 3 minutes. Lift out meat and set aside.

At once add celery, bell pepper, water chestnuts, onion, and hoisin. Stir-fry until vegetables are tender-crisp (2 to 3 more minutes). Return meat and any liquid to pan; stir until heated through. Serve immediately over hot cooked spinach. Makes 4 servings.

Arizona Fried Steak

A Western approach to chicken-fried steak

To complete the meal, we suggest hot cooked broccoli spears, cherry tomatoes, and crusty rolls.

> ½ cup masa harina or all-purpose flour
> ½ teaspoon *each* ground cumin, oregano leaves, and garlic powder
> ¼ teaspoon *each* onion powder, salt, and pepper
> ⅛ teaspoon ground red pepper (cayenne)
> 1 egg
> 2 to 3 tablespoons salad oil
> 1 can (7 oz.) green chile salsa
> 2 beef cube steaks (¾ to 1 lb. *total*)

In a rimmed plate or pie pan, stir together masa, cumin, oregano, garlic powder, onion powder, salt, pepper, and red pepper. In another rimmed plate or pie pan, beat egg until blended.

Heat 2 tablespoons of the oil in a wide frying pan over high heat. Meanwhile, pour salsa into a small pan and place over low heat. Dip each steak in egg; drain briefly, then coat completely with masa mixture, shaking off excess. Cook in hot oil until well browned on both sides but still pink in centers when slashed (3 to 4 minutes *total*), adding more oil as needed to prevent sticking.

Pour salsa into a small bowl and pass at the table to spoon over meat. Makes 2 servings.

Oven-roasted Prime Rib Bones

Have napkins handy to enjoy this finger-food spree

Pictured on facing page

To complete the meal, we suggest Peas in Pods (page 53), and Baked Potato Sticks (page 53).

> 3½ to 4 pounds standing rib bones
> ⅓ cup Dijon mustard
> 2 tablespoons red wine vinegar
> ¼ cup salad oil
> 1 clove garlic, minced or pressed
> ½ teaspoon *each* thyme leaves and Worcestershire
> ¼ teaspoon pepper
> Watercress and cherry peppers (optional)

Trim excess fat from meat and place ribs in a shallow roasting pan or broiler pan.

In a small bowl, stir together mustard and vinegar. Beating constantly with a wire whisk, slowly pour in oil. Then add garlic, thyme, Worcestershire, and pepper and beat until well blended. Generously brush about ⅔ of the mustard mixture over all sides of meat, then pierce meat all over with tines of a fork.

Roast, uncovered, in a 425° oven for 20 to 25 minutes for medium-rare, or until done to your liking when slashed; turn ribs over several times during roasting and baste with remaining mustard mixture. Cut into individual ribs; arrange on a platter and garnish with watercress and cherry peppers, if desired. Makes 3 or 4 servings.

Quick Flaky Piroshkis

Frozen patty shells streamline preparation

To complete the meal, we suggest hot onion soup, pickled beets, and sliced oranges.

> 1 package (10 oz.) frozen patty shells, thawed
> ½ pound lean ground beef
> 1 medium-size onion, chopped
> 2 cloves garlic, minced or pressed
> ¼ pound mushrooms, chopped
> 2 tablespoons soy sauce
> 2 hard-cooked eggs, chopped
> Pepper
> 1 egg white

Let patty shells thaw at room temperature.

Meanwhile, crumble beef into a wide frying pan over medium-high heat; cook, stirring often, until well browned (about 5 minutes). Add onion, garlic, and mushrooms and cook, stirring often, until onion is soft (about 10 more minutes). Stir in soy, scraping pan to loosen browned bits; remove from heat. Stir in eggs and season mixture to taste with pepper. Let cool.

On a lightly floured board, roll each shell out to a 7-inch circle; spoon ⅙ of the meat mixture onto center. Beat egg white lightly, then use to moisten edges of pastry. Bring edges to center and pinch firmly to seal; flute edge. Place piroshkis on an ungreased baking sheet, seam side up. Pierce tops in several places.

Bake, uncovered, in a 450° oven for about 20 minutes or until golden. Serve warm. Makes 6 servings.

Serve a feast of finger food with Oven-roasted Prime Rib Bones (recipe on this page), Peas in Pods (page 53), and Baked Potato Sticks (page 53). Offer ice cream cones for dessert.

Ground Beef Garden Sauté

Vary this dish with different garden vegetables

To complete the meal, we suggest a crisp green salad, steamed rice, and Fruit with Yogurt & Caramelized Sugar (page 92).

    ½ **cup slivered almonds**
    1 **pound lean ground beef**
    1 **medium-size onion, chopped**
    2 **cloves garlic, minced or pressed**
 1½ **cups thinly sliced green beans or zucchini, or whole edible-pod peas**
    4 **eggs**
      Soy sauce
    1 **teaspoon ground ginger**
    ½ **teaspoon dry mustard**
    ⅛ **teaspoon pepper**

Spread almonds in a shallow pan and toast in a 350° oven for about 6 minutes or until golden. Set aside.

Crumble beef into a wide frying pan over medium heat and cook, stirring often, until browned. Add onion and garlic and cook until onion is soft. Add green beans; cook, stirring often, until just tender (3 to 5 minutes).

In a small bowl, beat eggs slightly; then beat in 1 tablespoon soy, ginger, mustard, and pepper. Pour egg mixture over meat and cook until egg is set to your liking, lifting and turning mixture to cook it evenly. Top with almonds; pass additional soy at the table. Makes 4 servings.

Sour Cream Hamburgers

Creamy onion sauce tops open-faced hamburgers

To complete the meal, we suggest sliced tomatoes on lettuce, dill pickle spears, and fresh fruit.

    1 **pound lean ground beef**
    ½ **cup finely chopped onion**
    ⅓ **cup sour cream**
    ¼ **cup fine dry bread crumbs**
    1 **teaspoon Worcestershire**
    ½ **teaspoon dry basil**
    ¼ **teaspoon** *each* **salt and pepper**
      Sour Cream Sauce (recipe follows)
    2 **English muffins, split and toasted**

In a bowl, combine beef, onion, sour cream, bread crumbs, Worcestershire, basil, salt, and

pepper. Shape into 4 patties, *each* about 1 inch thick.

Arrange patties on a greased rack in a broiler pan. Broil 3 to 4 inches below heat for 5 minutes; turn over and broil for 3 to 5 more minutes for medium-rare; for more well-done meat, continue to cook, checking at 1 to 2-minute intervals, until done to your liking when slashed.

Meanwhile, prepare Sour Cream Sauce. Arrange each patty on a muffin half; spoon sauce evenly over top. Makes 4 servings.

Sour Cream Sauce. In a small pan, stir together 1 teaspoon **all-purpose flour** and ⅔ cup **sour cream** until smooth. Dissolve 1 **beef bouillon cube** in ¼ cup **hot water;** gradually stir into sour cream mixture. Add 2 tablespoons thinly sliced **green onion** (including top) and 1 tablespoon chopped **parsley.** Season to taste with **pepper.** Place over medium heat and cook, stirring occasionally, until bubbly.

Mexican Beef Bake

Individual casseroles make serving quick and easy

To complete the meal, we suggest sliced oranges, additional warm tortillas with butter, and a dry red wine.

    1 **pound lean ground beef**
    1 **large onion, chopped**
    1 **clove garlic, minced or pressed**
    ½ **cup catsup**
    1 **tablespoon chili powder**
      Salt and pepper
      About 2 tablespoons butter or margarine
    1 **egg**
    4 **corn tortillas**
 1½ **cups (6 oz.) shredded jack cheese**
    1 **avocado**
      Sour cream

Crumble beef into a wide frying pan over medium-high heat; cook, stirring often, until browned. Add onion and garlic and cook until onion is soft; spoon off and discard any fat, then stir in catsup and chili powder. Season to taste with salt and pepper. Reduce heat and simmer, uncovered, for 5 minutes.

Meanwhile, in a 7-inch frying pan over medium heat, melt about ½ tablespoon of the butter. In a rimmed plate or pie pan, beat egg just until blended. Dip 1 tortilla in egg and drain briefly; then cook in butter until lightly browned on both sides. Repeat with remaining tortillas, adding more butter as needed. Cut each tortilla into 4 wedges and arrange, pointed ends up, in a 1-cup ramekin. Spoon meat mixture over tortillas, then evenly sprinkle with cheese.

Broil 3 to 4 inches below heat until cheese is melted. Peel, pit, and slice avocado; top each serving with avocado slices and a dollop of sour cream. Makes 4 servings.

Peppered Chopped Steak

Beef patties crusted with pungent cracked pepper

To complete the meal, we suggest buttered carrots, toasted English muffin halves, and Fresh Raspberry Sundaes (page 92).

- 1½ **pounds lean ground beef**
- ⅓ **cup chopped parsley**
- 2 **cloves garlic, minced or pressed**
- ½ **teaspoon salt**
- 1 **tablespoon cracked black pepper**
- 2 **tablespoons butter or margarine**
- 8 to 10 **large mushrooms**
- 1 **tablespoon salad oil**
- ¾ **cup** *each* **regular-strength beef broth and whipping cream**
- 2 **tablespoons brandy (optional)**
  Watercress or parsley sprigs

In a bowl, combine beef, parsley, garlic, and salt; mix well and shape into 4 patties, *each* about 1 inch thick.

Sprinkle pepper on wax paper; turn patties in pepper to coat both sides evenly, pressing pepper in lightly.

In a wide frying pan over medium-high heat, melt 1 tablespoon of the butter. Add mushrooms and cook, stirring, until lightly browned (about 5 minutes). Transfer mushrooms to a platter; keep warm.

Add oil and remaining 1 tablespoon butter to pan. Place patties in pan and cook until well browned on the outside and done to your liking when slashed (6 to 10 minutes *total* for rare). Lift patties from pan and arrange on platter with mushrooms; keep warm.

Add broth to pan and bring to a boil. Boil, uncovered, scraping pan to loosen browned bits, until reduced by half. Add cream and brandy (if used), and boil, stirring, until sauce is slightly thickened. Pour sauce over patties and mushrooms. Garnish with watercress. Makes 4 servings.

Liver on Crisp Potato Pancake

Saucy liver strips on a skillet-size pancake

To complete the meal, we suggest crisp raw vegetables, olives, pickles, and chocolate sundaes.

- 4 **strips bacon**
- 1 **pound russet potatoes**
- 1 **tablespoon all-purpose flour**
- 4 **tablespoons butter or margarine**
- ½ **pound calf's liver, cut into ¼-inch strips**
- 2 **teaspoons Dijon mustard**
- ¼ **cup** *each* **whipping cream and finely chopped parsley**
  Lemon wedges
  Salt and pepper

In a wide frying pan with a nonstick finish, cook bacon over medium-low heat until crisp; remove from pan, drain, crumble, and set aside. Pour off and reserve drippings.

Peel potatoes and coarsely shred into a bowl of cold water; stir gently, then drain well. Mix flour into drained potatoes.

In the same pan over medium heat, melt 1 tablespoon of the butter. Add potatoes and pat into an even layer. Cover and cook for 5 minutes. Uncover and cook, pressing to compact into a solid layer, until well browned on bottom. Slide potato cake onto a rimless baking sheet. Melt 1 more tablespoon butter in pan; invert cake back into pan. Cook until browned on bottom, then slide onto a warm serving plate and keep hot.

Add 1 teaspoon of the reserved drippings to pan. Add half the liver and cook, turning as needed, until browned but still pink in center when slashed (about 1 minute). Remove from pan and place on a plate. Repeat with remaining liver; set liver aside.

Add 2 more tablespoons drippings, remaining 2 tablespoons butter, mustard, and cream to pan. Increase heat to high; cook and stir until sauce forms large, shiny bubbles. Stir any liver juices collected on plate into sauce; boil until thickened. Add liver and parsley; stir just until heated through.

Spoon liver mixture over pancake; top with bacon and garnish with lemon wedges. Season to taste with salt and pepper. Makes 3 or 4 servings.

Sweet & Sour Pork

A colorful version of a popular Chinese dish

To complete the meal, we suggest steamed rice and a mandarin orange and butter lettuce salad.

>   Sweet & Sour Sauce (recipe follows)
> 1 egg
> 2 pounds lean boneless pork, cut into 1-inch cubes
>   About ½ cup cornstarch
>   About 5 tablespoons salad oil
> 1 medium-size onion, cut into 1-inch squares
> 2 medium-size carrots, cut diagonally into ¼-inch slices
> 1 clove garlic, minced or pressed
> 1 large green pepper, seeded and cut into 1-inch squares
> ½ cup canned pineapple chunks in their own juice, drained well
> 2 medium-size tomatoes, cut into 1-inch cubes

Prepare Sweet & Sour Sauce; set aside.

In a rimmed plate or pie pan, beat egg just until blended. Dip pork pieces in egg and drain briefly; then roll in cornstarch until lightly coated on all sides, shaking off excess. Heat a wok or wide frying pan over medium-high heat. Add about 3 tablespoons of the oil; when oil is hot, add pork. Stir-fry until browned (about 7 minutes); lift out and set aside. Scrape free and discard any browned bits clinging to pan; leave oil in pan.

Add enough of the remaining oil to pan to make about 2 tablespoons *total*; place over high heat. Add onion, carrots, and garlic and stir-fry for about 3 minutes. Add green pepper, pineapple, tomatoes, and Sweet & Sour Sauce; cook, stirring, until mixture boils. Add pork and cook, stirring, until pork is heated through and coated with sauce (about 1 more minute). Makes 6 servings.

Sweet & Sour Sauce. In a bowl, stir together 1 tablespoon **cornstarch**, ⅓ cup firmly packed **brown sugar**, ¼ teaspoon **ground ginger**, 1 tablespoon *each* **soy sauce** and **dry sherry**, and ¼ cup *each* **white wine vinegar** and **regular-strength chicken broth**.

A treat for the eyes as well as the palate, Smoked Pork Chops with Curried New Potatoes & Green Beans (page 84) is a study in contrasting shapes, colors, flavors, and textures.

Pork Scallopini with Mustard Cream

Four-step scallopini: pound, flour, sauté, and sauce

To complete the meal, we suggest hot buttered spinach, crusty rolls, and a dry white wine.

Hint for the cook: If you prefer, use veal instead of pork.

>   About ¾ pound shoulder, loin, or leg pork chops or steaks, cut about ½ inch thick
>   All-purpose flour
> 2 to 3 tablespoons butter or margarine
> 2 to 3 tablespoons salad oil
> ⅓ cup dry vermouth
> ¼ cup whipping cream
> 1 tablespoon Dijon mustard
>   Dash of ground nutmeg
>   Salt and pepper
>   Chopped parsley

Cut away and discard any bones and fat from meat. Following natural divisions, separate large steaks into smaller pieces. Place meat between sheets of wax paper and, using a heavy wooden mallet, pound evenly and gently until about ¼ inch thick.

Coat meat with flour, shaking off excess. In a wide frying pan over medium-high heat, melt 1 tablespoon of the butter in 1 tablespoon of the oil; when hot, add as many meat pieces as will fit without crowding. Cook, turning once, just until lightly browned and no longer pink in centers when slashed (about 3 minutes *total*). Place on a hot platter and keep warm. Cook remaining pieces, adding more butter and oil as needed to prevent sticking.

Pour vermouth into pan and stir, scraping bottom of pan to loosen browned bits. Bring to a boil; boil until reduced by about half. Stir in cream, mustard, and nutmeg. Return to boil and cook, stirring, until slightly thickened. Stir any meat juices collected on platter into sauce; season to taste with salt and pepper. Pour sauce over meat; garnish with chopped parsley. Makes 2 servings.

Lemon-Thyme Chicken Scallopini

Follow directions for **Pork Scallopini with Mustard Cream,** using 4 large **chicken thighs** (skinned and boned) instead of pork. Substitute **dry white wine** or regular-strength chicken broth for vermouth. Omit mustard and nutmeg; instead, use 1 teaspoon **lemon juice** and ¼ teaspoon **thyme leaves.**

Glazed Pork Tenderloin

Roast pork for two, with little effort

To complete the meal, we suggest cooked baby carrots, warm dinner rolls, and chilled melon.

> 2 teaspoons brown sugar
> 1 teaspoon cornstarch
>   About ½ cup whipping cream
> 1 teaspoon *each* soy sauce and lemon juice
> 1 whole pork tenderloin (about 12 oz.)
>   Chopped parsley

In a small pan, stir together sugar and cornstarch; slowly stir in ½ cup of the cream. Place pan over medium-high heat; cook, stirring constantly, until mixture boils. Stir in soy and lemon juice and remove from heat.

Place pork in a shallow baking pan, then place in a 425° oven. Roast, uncovered, for 25 to 30 minutes or until meat in thickest portion is no longer pink when slashed; brush cream mixture over pork frequently during roasting.

Transfer pork to a warm platter; sprinkle with parsley and keep warm. Pour remaining cream mixture into baking pan; place over medium heat and cook until heated through, scraping pan to loosen browned bits. Stir in any meat juices collected on platter; then add more cream to thin sauce to desired consistency. Pour into a bowl and pass at the table. Makes 2 servings.

Baked Pork Chops with Caper Sauce

Simple caper sauce enhances pork chops

To complete the meal, we suggest Skillet Squash (page 53), rice, and your favorite beverage.

> 4 loin pork chops, cut 1 inch thick
> 3 tablespoons all-purpose flour
> 2 tablespoons salad oil
> ½ cup regular-strength beef broth
> 2 teaspoons Dijon mustard
> 2 to 3 teaspoons capers, drained well
> 2 tablespoons water
> ½ cup sour cream
>   Salt and pepper
>   Parsley sprigs

Coat chops on all sides with 2 tablespoons of the flour, shaking off excess. Heat oil in a wide frying pan over medium-high heat; add chops and cook until browned on all sides. Transfer chops to a 9-inch square baking pan. In a glass measuring cup, stir together broth, mustard, and capers; pour over chops. Cover and bake in a 350° oven for 25 to 30 minutes or until no longer pink when slashed. Remove to a warm platter; keep warm. Reserve pan juices.

Meanwhile, discard fat in frying pan. Add remaining 1 tablespoon flour to pan, then stir in water until blended. Stir in sour cream. Blend in reserved juices from chops and cook over medium-high heat, stirring, until sauce boils. Season to taste with salt and pepper. Pour some of the sauce over chops; garnish with parsley. Serve remaining sauce in a bowl to spoon over rice. Makes 4 servings.

Smoked Pork Chops with Curried New Potatoes & Green Beans

A good choice for guests when time is short

Pictured on page 82

To complete the meal, we suggest a fruit sherbet and butter cookies, and your favorite beverage.

> 10 to 12 red thin-skinned potatoes (*each* about 2 inches in diameter)
> 1 pound green beans, ends removed
> 6 tablespoons butter or margarine
> 6 smoked pork chops, cut ¾ inch thick
> 2 tablespoons whole mustard seeds
> 2 teaspoons curry powder

Scrub potatoes, but do not peel. Place on a steaming rack over boiling water, in a large kettle; cover and steam for 15 minutes. Add beans to rack; cover and steam until potatoes and beans are tender (about 10 more minutes).

While potatoes are cooking, melt about 2 teaspoons of the butter in a wide frying pan over medium heat. Add chops, three at a time, and cook, turning once, until lightly browned on both sides (about 10 minutes *total*). Arrange chops on a platter; keep warm.

Add remaining butter to pan. When butter is melted, stir in mustard seeds and curry powder. Cut potatoes in half; add to pan, cut side down, and cook until lightly browned (about 5 minutes). Lift out and arrange with chops on platter. Add beans to pan, turn to coat in butter, and heat through; arrange on platter. Drizzle vegetables with remaining butter mixture. Makes 6 servings.

Wurst & Cabbage Plate

Fresh orange accents richly glazed garlic franks

To complete the meal, we suggest a dark rye bread with sweet butter, or your favorite potato salad.

    1 to 1½ pounds knackwurst (garlic frankfurters)
    ¼ cup *each* honey and soy sauce
    3 tablespoons tomato-based chili sauce
    1 tablespoon cider vinegar
    ¼ teaspoon garlic powder
    1 small head cabbage
    3 to 4 tablespoons butter or margarine
      Salt, pepper, and dill weed
    2 medium-size unpeeled oranges, cut
      into wedges

Cut ¼-inch-deep slashes into each sausage at about 1-inch intervals. Place sausages in a wide frying pan over medium heat and cook, turning as needed, until lightly browned on all sides. In a glass measuring cup, stir together honey, soy, chili sauce, vinegar, and garlic powder; pour into pan and continue to cook, stirring often, until sauce is slightly thickened and sausages are well glazed (about 5 minutes).

Meanwhile, cut cabbage into quarters; cut out and discard core from each quarter. Pour water into a wide frying pan to a depth of 1 inch; bring to a boil over high heat. Add cabbage; then cover, reduce heat to medium, and cook until cabbage is just tender when pierced (about 8 minutes). Meanwhile, in a small pan, melt butter. Drain cabbage well, drizzle butter evenly over top, and season to taste with salt, pepper, and dill.

Arrange a cabbage wedge, 1 or 2 sausages, and several orange wedges on each plate; pass remaining sauce to spoon over sausages. Makes 4 servings.

Apricot-glazed Baked Ham

Ham and a fruity glaze are natural partners

To complete the meal, we suggest crisp coleslaw, warm cornbread, and iced tea.

    1 can (1½ lbs.) fully cooked ham
    ¼ cup apricot preserves
    1 tablespoon dry sherry
    1 teaspoon lemon juice
    ¼ teaspoon ground cinnamon

Place ham in a baking pan; bake, uncovered, in a 325° oven for 20 minutes. Meanwhile, stir together preserves, sherry, lemon juice, and cinnamon.

Remove ham from oven; cut diagonal slashes in top of ham, then brush evenly with some of the preserves mixture. Return to oven and bake for 25 to 30 more minutes, basting with remaining mixture after 15 minutes. Makes 4 to 6 servings.

Mustard-glazed Baked Ham

Follow directions for **Apricot-glazed Baked Ham,** but omit preserves, sherry, lemon juice, and cinnamon. Instead, use ¼ cup *each* **pineapple juice** and firmly packed **brown sugar** and 1 tablespoon **Dijon mustard.**

Open-faced Franks

Ever-popular frankfurters dressed up for supper

To complete the meal, we suggest a sauerkraut salad and apple cider or cold beer.

    6 frankfurters
    2 tablespoons *each* sweet pickle relish,
      drained well, and Dijon mustard
    1 cup all-purpose flour
    ½ cup yellow cornmeal
    2 teaspoons sugar
    1½ teaspoons baking powder
    1 tablespoon finely chopped green onion
      (including top)
    ½ teaspoon oregano leaves
    ¼ teaspoon salt
    1 egg
    ½ cup milk
    3 tablespoons butter or margarine, melted
    ½ cup shredded sharp Cheddar cheese

Without cutting all the way through, split frankfurters lengthwise. Combine relish and mustard and spread down centers of frankfurters.

Stir together flour, cornmeal, sugar, baking powder, onion, oregano, and salt. Combine egg, milk, and butter; beat into flour mixture.

Spread dough in a greased 7 by 11-inch baking pan. Arrange frankfurters, cut side up, slightly apart down length of pan, pressing slightly into dough. Sprinkle evenly with cheese.

Bake, uncovered, in a 400° oven for about 25 minutes or until a wooden pick inserted in dough comes out clean. Cut between frankfurters and lift from pan. Makes 6 servings.

Lemon-Mint Lamb Meatballs

The flavors of Greece in a simple entrée

Pictured on facing page

To complete the meal, we suggest Cream-glazed Anise Carrots (page 52), warm bread, and white wine.

2 pounds lean ground lamb
2 eggs
¼ cup all-purpose flour
1 tablespoon crumbled dry mint
1 teaspoon *each* salt and pepper
2 tablespoons salad oil
⅓ cup finely chopped parsley
1¾ cups thinly sliced green onions (including tops)
   Hot cooked rice
1 can (14½ oz.) regular-strength chicken broth
⅓ cup lemon juice
1 tablespoon *each* cornstarch and water
   Lemon zest and fresh mint sprigs

In a large bowl, combine lamb, eggs, flour, mint, salt, and pepper; mix well, then shape into 1½-inch balls. Set slightly apart on an ungreased large rimmed baking sheet. Bake in a 500° oven for 10 minutes or until well browned.

Meanwhile, heat oil in a wide frying pan over medium heat; add parsley and 1½ cups of the onions and cook, stirring often, until onions are soft. Remove pan from heat.

With a slotted spoon, arrange meatballs over a bed of hot cooked rice on a serving dish; keep warm. Drain off and discard fat from baking pan. Pour a small amount of the broth into pan and scrape to loosen browned bits; then pour into frying pan and add remaining broth and lemon juice. Place pan over medium-high heat. In a small bowl, mix cornstarch and water; stir into broth mixture and cook, stirring, until thickened. Pour sauce over meatballs and garnish with remaining onions, lemon zest, and mint. Makes 6 servings.

Mediterranean Meatballs

Follow directions for **Lemon-Mint Lamb Meatballs,** using either **lean ground beef** or lean ground lamb. Substitute **fine dry bread crumbs** for the flour. Omit mint; instead, use 2 teaspoons **oregano leaves,** ½ teaspoon **ground cumin,** and 1 clove **garlic** (minced or pressed).

Pan-broiled Lamb Chops or Steaks

Piquant marinade turns into a quick sauce

To complete the meal, we suggest Asparagus with Cashew Butter (page 52), hot biscuits, and Pineapple with Sour Cream Topping (page 92).

Hint for the cook: The longer the lamb marinates, the better the flavor. If you have time, let it marinate (covered) in the refrigerator for 4 to 6 hours—or until the next day.

4 loin or rib lamb chops or 2 lamb leg steaks, cut about ¾ inch thick
½ cup cold strong coffee
¼ cup firmly packed brown sugar
1 tablespoon prepared mustard
½ teaspoon Worcestershire
2 tablespoons lemon juice
   Few drops of liquid hot pepper seasoning
1 clove garlic, minced or pressed
   Chopped parsley

Trim excess fat from chops; discard all but 1 piece of fat. Slash through remaining edge fat at 1-inch intervals, cutting to, but not into, meat. Place chops in a single layer in a shallow roasting pan. In a glass measuring cup, stir together coffee, sugar, mustard, Worcestershire, lemon juice, hot pepper seasoning, and garlic; pour over lamb. Let stand for 20 to 30 minutes, turning chops over several times.

In a wide frying pan over medium-high heat, swirl reserved piece of fat to grease pan bottom lightly; then discard fat. Lift chops from marinade, drain briefly (reserve marinade), and place in pan. Cook, turning as needed, until well browned on both sides but still pink in thickest portion when slashed (6 to 8 minutes *total*). Place chops on a warm platter; keep warm. Pour reserved marinade into pan; increase heat to high and cook until slightly thickened and reduced to about ⅓ cup. Pour sauce over chops and garnish with parsley. Makes 2 servings.

Greek cooks enhance their meatballs with the flavors of lemon and mint. You can do the same, to make a refreshingly different entrée—Lemon-Mint Lamb Meatballs (recipe on this page).

Quick Lamb Curry

Add cayenne pepper for curry as hot as you like it

To complete the meal, we suggest hot cooked rice, cherry tomatoes, and a fruit sherbet.

>   1 **pound lean ground lamb**
>   2 **cloves garlic, minced or pressed**
>   1 **large onion, chopped**
>   1 **tablespoon curry powder**
>   ½ **teaspoon** *each* **ground ginger and ground cumin**
>   1 **medium-size carrot, thinly sliced**
>   1 **small red apple, cored and chopped**
>   1 **small green pepper, seeded and chopped**
>   1 **can (14½ oz.) regular-strength beef broth**
>   **Salt and ground red pepper (cayenne)**
>   **Condiments: Sliced bananas, Major Grey chutney, plain yogurt, chopped peanuts, crumbled bacon**

Crumble lamb into a wide frying pan over medium heat; cook, stirring, until browned, then spoon off and discard all but 2 tablespoons fat. Add garlic, onion, curry powder, ginger, and cumin; reduce heat to low and cook, stirring often, until onion is very soft. Add carrot, apple, green pepper, and broth. Simmer, uncovered, until vegetables are tender and sauce is slightly thickened (about 20 minutes). Season to taste with salt and red pepper.

While curry is cooking, prepare 3 or 4 condiments of your choice and place each in a separate bowl; pass at the table to sprinkle over individual servings. Makes 4 servings.

Lamb Shish Kebabs

Skewered chunks of lamb and fresh vegetables

To complete the meal, we suggest a simple tomato-lettuce salad, with cheese and fruit for dessert.

>   1 **to 1½ pounds lean boneless lamb (shoulder or leg), cut into 1½-inch cubes**
>   **Lemon Marinade (recipe follows)**
>   1 **medium-size red or green bell pepper**
>   1 **medium-size white onion**
>   8 **medium-size mushrooms**

Trim and discard excess fat from meat; place meat in a bowl. Prepare Lemon Marinade and pour over meat; let stand for 15 to 20 minutes. Seed bell pepper and cut into 1½-inch squares; cut onion into 8 wedges and separate each into layers.

Remove meat from marinade, drain briefly (reserve marinade), and divide into 4 equal portions. Thread meat and vegetables alternately on four 10 to 12-inch skewers, starting and ending each skewer with a mushroom.

Place skewers on a greased rack in a broiler pan; broil 2½ to 3 inches below heat, turning as needed and basting frequently with reserved marinade, until meat is browned on all sides but still pink in center when slashed (10 to 15 minutes *total*). Makes 4 servings.

Lemon Marinade. In a small bowl, combine 2 tablespoons chopped **parsley,** ⅓ cup **salad oil,** 1 tablespoon **soy sauce,** ½ teaspoon *each* **dry mustard** and **Worcestershire,** ¼ cup **lemon juice,** and 1 clove **garlic** (minced or pressed).

Roast Rack of Lamb

An effortless, elegant entrée with roasted potatoes

To complete the meal, we suggest hot cooked green beans or asparagus, and a butter lettuce salad.

>   **Parsley Butter (recipe follows)**
>   1 **rack of lamb (2 to 2½ lbs.)**
>   4 **to 6 red thin-skinned potatoes (***each* **2 to 2½ inches in diameter)**

Prepare Parsley Butter and rub about 1½ tablespoons over all sides of lamb. Place meat, fat side up, in a shallow roasting pan; insert a meat thermometer in thickest part of roast (not touching bone). Pierce potatoes in several places; arrange in pan beside meat.

Roast, uncovered, in a 425° oven for 35 minutes or until meat thermometer reaches 145° for medium-rare, and potatoes feel soft when squeezed. If meat is done before potatoes, remove from pan and keep warm.

Cut lamb between ribs into individual chops; offer remaining Parsley Butter to top meat and potatoes. Makes 2 servings.

Parsley Butter. In a small bowl, combine 6 tablespoons **butter** or margarine (softened), ⅓ cup minced **parsley,** 1 clove **garlic** (minced or pressed), and ¼ teaspoon *each* **salt** and **pepper.**

Meat Broiling Made Easy

No matter which cut of beef or lamb you choose, the procedure for broiling is the same. The suggested cooking times that follow are for meat cooked rare or medium-rare; for more well-done meat, continue to cook, checking at 1 to 2-minute intervals, until meat is done to your liking when slashed. Serve broiled meats plain, or top them with a seasoned butter.

Cuts of meat

Best beef candidates for the broiler are tender steaks such as porterhouse, T-bone, club, rib, and top sirloin.

Less tender steaks, such as flank and top round, also broil well if you marinate them first and cook just to rare or medium-rare.

Several lamb cuts are suitable for broiling; your selection will probably depend on the occasion and your budget. For special occasions, choose tender cuts such as lamb steaks cut from the leg, small loin chops, or rib chops. For everyday meals, buy round bone or blade shoulder chops. If you need lamb cubes, use boneless lamb from the leg or shoulder.

Broiling techniques

Select a large, shallow pan with a rack and place the meat on the rack. Position the pan below the heat source in your broiler, adjusting the pan (or the rack on which the pan is resting) until the top of the meat is the recommended distance below the heat source.

Remove the meat from the broiler, leaving the pan and rack inside. Preheat the broiler for 5 to 7 minutes. Meanwhile, if the meat has a border of fat, slash through the fat at 1-inch intervals, cutting just to the lean meat, to prevent curling. Remove the pan from the broiler and lightly grease the hot rack.

Place the meat on the rack and broil, turning as needed, for the time specified in the following guide or until browned on all sides and done to your liking when slashed in thickest portion.

Cut	Thickness (in inches)	Distance Below Heat (in inches)	Approximate Total Cooking Time (in minutes)
BEEF			
Steaks	¾	3	6–8 (R)
			8–10 (MR)
	1	3	9–11 (R)
			11–12 (MR)
	1½	3	10–12 (R)
			12–14 (MR)
	2–2¼	3	20–22 (R)
			22–25 (MR)
Ground patties	¾–1	3–4	8–10 (MR)
LAMB			
Chops and steaks	¾	3	8–10 (MR)
	1	3	9–11 (MR)
	1½	3	11–13 (MR)
Cubes	1½	2½–3	10–15 (MR)
Ground patties	¾–1	4–6	8–12 (MW)

(R) Rare   (MR) Medium-rare   (MW) Medium-well

Seasoned butters

These butters keep well in the refrigerator for up to 2 weeks.

Fresh Herb Butter. In a bowl, combine ½ cup (¼ lb.) **butter** or margarine (softened); ½ cup lightly packed **fresh basil,** chives, mint, parsley, or watercress (minced); and 1 teaspoon **lemon juice.** Beat until blended. Makes about ½ cup.

Lemon Butter. In a bowl, combine 1 cup (½ lb.) **butter** or margarine (softened), 2 teaspoons grated **lemon peel,** ⅓ cup chopped **parsley,** 1 teaspoon **dry tarragon,** and 3 tablespoons **lemon juice;** beat until blended. Makes about 1 cup.

Cheese-crusted Veal Patties

Moist patties with crunchy Parmesan coating

To complete the meal, we suggest Cream-glazed Anise Carrots (page 52) and a spinach salad.

- 1 pound lean ground veal
- ½ cup *each* fine dry bread crumbs and grated Parmesan cheese
- 2 eggs
- ½ teaspoon *each* salt and oregano leaves
- ¼ teaspoon pepper
- ⅛ teaspoon garlic powder
- 2 tablespoons *each* dry white wine and finely chopped green onion (including top)
  About ¼ cup all-purpose flour
- 2 tablespoons salad oil

In a large bowl, combine veal, ¼ cup *each* of the bread crumbs and cheese, 1 of the eggs, salt, oregano, pepper, garlic powder, wine, and onion. Shape mixture into 4 patties, *each* ¾ to 1 inch thick.

In a rimmed plate or pie pan, beat remaining egg just until blended. In separate rimmed plates or pie pans, place remaining ¼ cup *each* bread crumbs and cheese (stirred together) and flour. Coat each patty with flour, shaking off excess; dip in egg to cover, then coat completely with crumb mixture.

Heat oil in a wide frying pan over medium heat; add patties and cook until browned on both sides and no longer pink in centers when slashed (10 to 15 minutes *total*). Makes 4 servings.

Skillet Grill

Simple solution to leftover veal or beef roast

To complete the meal, we suggest buttered cauliflower sprinkled with dill weed, and crusty rolls.

- 3 tablespoons butter or margarine
- 2 tablespoons Dijon mustard
- 1 pound sliced cooked veal or beef
  Thinly sliced green onions (including tops)

In a wide frying pan over medium-low heat, melt butter; stir in mustard. Spread mixture evenly over bottom of pan. Arrange meat in pan and cook, turning as needed, until lightly browned on both sides and heated through. Transfer to a platter and garnish with onions. Makes 4 servings.

Veal & Asparagus Platter

Distinctive sauce unites sautéed veal, vegetables

To complete the meal, we suggest boiled red thin-skinned potatoes and a tossed green salad.

- 1½ pounds lean boneless veal, cut into ½-inch-thick slices
  Salt and pepper
  All-purpose flour
  About 4 tablespoons butter or margarine
  About 2 tablespoons salad oil
- 2 pounds asparagus
- ½ pound mushrooms, sliced
- 2 tablespoons brandy (optional)
- ½ teaspoon *each* dry tarragon and dry mustard
- ⅔ cup half-and-half (light cream)
- 1 tablespoon lemon juice

Trim and discard any fat and membrane from veal; sprinkle lightly with salt and pepper and dust with flour, shaking off excess. In a wide frying pan over medium heat, melt 1 tablespoon of the butter in 1 tablespoon of the oil; when hot, add about ⅓ of the veal and cook until well browned on both sides and no longer pink in center when slashed (about 10 minutes *total*). Transfer to a warm serving platter; keep warm. Cook remaining veal in 2 portions, adding more butter and oil as needed to prevent sticking.

Meanwhile, snap off and discard tough ends of asparagus; rinse. In a wide frying pan or kettle, immerse spears in 1½ inches boiling water and cook, uncovered, just until tender (5 to 7 minutes). Drain well; arrange on platter with veal.

In frying pan used for veal, over medium heat, melt 2 more tablespoons butter; add mushrooms and cook until lightly browned. Stir in 1 tablespoon flour; cook, stirring, for 1 minute. In a small pan over low heat, warm brandy (if used), ignite, and pour into frying pan. When flames disappear, add tarragon, mustard, and half-and-half. Cook, stirring, until bubbly and thickened. Remove from heat, stir in lemon juice, and pour over veal and asparagus. Makes 6 servings.

Italian Veal with Peppers

For extra color, use red and green peppers

To complete the meal, we suggest corn on the cob, a marinated bean salad, and dry white wine.

> 1 **pound lean boneless veal, cut into ³/₁₆-inch-thick slices**
> **All-purpose flour**
> **About 3 tablespoons butter or margarine**
> **About 3 tablespoons salad oil**
> 2 **large red or green bell peppers (or 1 of each), seeded and cut into ½-inch-wide strips**
> 1 **teaspoon oregano leaves**
> 1 **clove garlic, minced or pressed**
> ⅔ **cup dry white wine**
> **Salt and pepper**

Trim and discard any fat and membrane from veal; cut meat into pieces about 3 inches square. Dredge veal squares in flour to coat lightly, shaking off excess; set aside.

In a wide frying pan over medium heat, melt 1 tablespoon of the butter in 1 tablespoon of the oil; add bell pepper strips, oregano, and garlic and cook, stirring, until peppers are soft (about 5 minutes). With a slotted spoon, transfer pepper mixture to a serving dish; keep warm.

Increase heat to medium-high; add 1 more tablespoon *each* butter and oil. When butter mixture is hot, add about ⅓ of the veal and cook just until lightly browned on both sides (1½ to 2 minutes *total*). Arrange cooked veal in dish with peppers; cook remaining veal in 2 portions, adding more butter and oil as needed to prevent sticking.

Add wine to pan; bring to a boil. Boil, scraping pan to loosen browned bits, until liquid is reduced by about half. Season to taste with salt and pepper; pour over veal. Makes 4 servings.

Sesame Veal

Sesame butter adds special richness and flavor

To complete the meal, we suggest sliced tomatoes and cucumbers, and hot cooked lima beans.

> 4 **loin veal chops, cut about ¾ inch thick**
> **Pepper**
> 5 **tablespoons butter or margarine**
> 1 **tablespoon dry white wine**
> 3 to 4 **teaspoons sesame seeds**
> ½ **teaspoon grated lemon peel**

Sprinkle chops with pepper. In a wide frying pan over medium-high heat, melt 1 tablespoon of the butter; add chops and wine, then cover and cook for 4 minutes. Uncover and continue cooking, turning once, until chops are browned on both sides and no longer pink in centers when slashed (5 to 8 minutes *total*).

Meanwhile, place sesame seeds in a small pan over medium-high heat; cook, stirring often, until seeds are richly browned. Add remaining 4 tablespoons butter and lemon peel; remove from heat and stir until butter is melted.

Transfer chops to a platter and pour sesame butter over top. Makes 4 servings.

Lemon-glazed Veal Chops

Delicate veal simmers in subtle sweet-sour sauce

To complete the meal, we suggest noodles dressed with parsley butter, and hot cooked peas.

> 4 **shoulder or loin veal chops, cut about 1 inch thick**
> **Pepper**
> 2 **tablespoons salad oil**
> 1 **small onion, finely chopped**
> 2 **tablespoons vinegar**
> ½ **teaspoon ground ginger**
> 3 **tablespoons firmly packed brown sugar**
> 1 **bay leaf**
> 10 **thin lemon slices**
> 2 **beef bouillon cubes**
> ¼ **cup water**

Sprinkle chops with pepper. Heat oil in a wide frying pan over medium-high heat; add chops and cook until browned on both sides. Remove from pan and set aside.

Add onion to pan and cook, stirring, until soft. Stir in vinegar, ginger, sugar, bay leaf, 6 of the lemon slices, bouillon cubes, and water. Bring to a boil; then return chops to pan, reduce heat, cover, and simmer until chops are tender when pierced (about 20 minutes). Turn chops over several times to cook them evenly.

Arrange chops on a platter. Discard bay leaf and lemon slices from pan; spoon sauce evenly over chops and garnish with remaining 4 lemon slices. Makes 4 servings.

Quick Dessert Ideas

For some, dinner isn't dinner without a dessert. For others, dessert is simply a welcome treat. For the cook, though, a sweet ending can be a way to transform an otherwise light offering into a satisfying meal.

When time is short, scoops of ice cream or seasonal fresh fruits are popular choices. But when you pair ice cream or fruit with a noteworthy sauce or topping, you can quickly create a memorable dessert. Here, we suggest several such combinations. Or try our berry slush, luscious chocolate fondue, or cooky-like treats made from tortillas.

Spiced Almonds & Melon

Place ½ cup **blanched whole almonds** in a shallow baking pan. Bake in a 350° oven, shaking pan occasionally to turn nuts, for about 10 minutes or until golden; let cool completely. In a blender or food processor, place almonds, 2 tablespoons **sugar,** and ¼ teaspoon **ground nutmeg.** Whirl until almonds are finely ground. Arrange 4 wedges of **cantaloupe** or Persian or Crenshaw melon on individual plates; sprinkle nut mixture evenly over top. Makes 4 servings.

Pineapple with Sour Cream Topping

Remove rind and core from 1 large **pineapple** (about 4½ lbs.); cut fruit into bite-size chunks and place in a serving bowl.

Stir together ⅔ cup **sour cream** and 1 tablespoon **brown sugar;** spoon over pineapple. Just before serving, sprinkle with ⅓ cup *each* chopped **salted peanuts** and **shredded coconut.** Makes 4 servings.

Fruit with Yogurt & Caramelized Sugar

Rinse and dry 6 to 8 large **strawberries** and remove stems; or cut 4 small apricots in half and remove pits; or peel 2 small peaches, cut in half, and remove pits. Divide 1 carton (8 oz.) **vanilla-flavored yogurt** between 2 small shallow serving bowls. Set 3 or 4 berries, 4 apricot halves, or 2 peach halves on each portion.

Place about 1½ tablespoons **sugar** in a 6-inch frying pan. Set over medium heat and shake pan to mix sugar as it begins to liquefy and caramelize. When sugar is liquid and amber (do not let sugar scorch), let cool just until thickened to the consistency of light syrup (about 1 minute); then drizzle over fruit and yogurt. Makes 2 servings.

Figs Romanoff

In the top of a double boiler, beat 6 **egg yolks** until frothy; then beat in ¾ cup **sugar** and ¼ cup **rum.** Place over simmering water and cook, stirring constantly, until mixture is slightly thickened. Immediately remove from heat and let cool.

While mixture cools, rinse and slice 10 to 12 **figs.** In a small bowl, beat 1 cup **whipping cream** until soft peaks form; fold in cooled rum mixture, then spoon into 6 to 8 small individual serving dishes and top with figs. Makes 6 to 8 servings.

Cream Sundaes

In a small bowl, beat ½ cup **whipping cream** until it holds soft peaks; stir in 1 tablespoon **powdered sugar** and ¼ teaspoon **vanilla.**

Divide about 1 pint **vanilla ice cream** among 4 sherbet glasses; over each, spoon an equal amount of **chestnut pieces in vanilla syrup** or preserved ginger in syrup (use about ½ cup *total*). Top each sundae with some of the whipped cream and 1 tablespoon coarsely grated **bittersweet chocolate.** Makes 4 servings.

Fresh Raspberry Sundaes

In a 2-quart pan, stir together ½ cup **sugar** and 1 tablespoon **cornstarch.** Rinse 2 cups raspberries; add about half the berries to cornstarch mixture and crush them with a spoon. Place over medium heat and cook, stirring, until sauce boils and thickens. Remove from heat; stir in remaining berries, 1 tablespoon **lemon juice,** and ¼ teaspoon **ground cinnamon.** Let cool.

Scoop 1 to 1½ pints **toasted almond ice cream** into 4 sherbet glasses; spoon raspberry sauce over top. Makes 4 servings.

Fresh Peach Sundaes with Hot Chocolate Sauce

In a small pan over lowest possible heat, place 4 ounces **semisweet chocolate,** coarsely chopped, and 6 tablespoons **whipping cream.** Stir constantly until chocolate is melted and well blended with cream; keep warm.

Halve, pit, and peel 2 large ripe **peaches;** place each half in a sherbet glass and top with a scoop of **vanilla ice cream** (you'll need about 1 pint *total*). Drizzle warm sauce evenly over top. Serve immediately. Makes 4 servings.

Berry Slush

In a food processor or blender, place ⅓ cup **whipping cream** or half-and-half (light cream). With motor running, add 3 cups **unsweetened frozen blackberries** or raspberries, about ¼ cup at a time, until smoothly blended. (If you're using a blender, you may need to add 2 to 4 tablespoons more cream.) Mix in 3 to 4 tablespoons **sugar,** or to taste. Spoon into 4 glasses; serve immediately (or, if a thicker consistency is desired, place in the freezer for a few minutes). Makes 4 servings.

Blazing Bananas

Spread 4 to 6 tablespoons **sliced almonds** in a shallow baking pan. Place in a 350° oven and bake for about 6 minutes or until golden. Set aside.

Cut 4 to 6 medium-size firm-ripe **bananas** in half lengthwise, then crosswise.

Dip each banana quarter in **lemon juice** to prevent browning, then set aside. In a small bowl, beat ½ cup **whipping cream** until soft peaks form; set aside.

In a wide frying pan over medium heat, combine ⅓ cup firmly packed **brown sugar** and ⅓ cup **butter** or margarine; heat until bubbly. Add bananas; cook until heated through (3 to 5 minutes), turning gently to coat evenly with glaze. In a small pan over low heat, warm ⅓ cup **coffee-flavored liqueur;** pour over bananas and ignite. When flames die, spoon bananas and some of the glaze into 4 to 6 individual serving dishes. Top each with a dollop of whipped cream; sprinkle with almonds. Makes 4 to 6 servings.

Chocolate Fondue

In a small pan or fondue pot over lowest possible heat, place 4 ounces **semisweet chocolate,** coarsely chopped, and 6 tablespoons **whipping cream.** Stir constantly until chocolate is melted and well blended with cream. Stir in 4 teaspoons **rum** or 1 teaspoon rum flavoring; keep warm.

Cut 4 large firm-ripe **pears** into wedges; cut out cores and peel, if desired. Also cut 4 to 6 slices **pound cake** (each 1 to 1½ inches thick) into cubes.

Place pan of sauce over canned heat to keep warm; offer pears and cake to dip in hot sauce. (Use fondue forks or bamboo skewers to spear cake.) Makes 4 servings.

Tortilla Crisps

In a small bowl, stir together ⅓ cup **sugar** and 1½ teaspoons **ground cinnamon;** set aside.

Into a wide frying pan, pour **salad oil** to a depth of ½ inch and heat over medium-high heat to 350°. Add 10 to 12 **flour tortillas** (whole or cut into wedges), one at a time, and cook until golden and puffy (about 30 seconds on each side); drain on paper towels. Lightly sprinkle one side of each hot tortilla with cinnamon-sugar mixture. Makes 10 to 12 servings.

Index

Metric Conversion Table

To change	To	Multiply by
ounces (oz.)	grams (g)	28
pounds (lbs.)	kilograms (kg)	0.45
teaspoons	milliliters (ml)	5
tablespoons	milliliters (ml)	15
fluid ounces (fl. oz.)	milliliters (ml)	30
cups	liters (l)	0.24
pints (pt.)	liters (l)	0.47
quarts (qt.)	liters (l)	0.95
gallons (gal.)	liters (l)	3.8
Fahrenheit temperature (°F)	Celsius temperature (°C)	5/9 after subtracting 32